Literary Theory

GUIDES TO
THEOLOGICAL
INQUIRY

Edited by Kathryn Tanner of the University of Chicago
and Paul Lakeland of Fairfield University, *Guides to
Theological Inquiry* are intended to introduce theologians,
scholars, students, and clergy to those academic methods,
disciplines, and movements that are most germane to contemporary theology. Neither simple surveys nor exhaustive
monographs, these short books will provide solid, reliable,
programmatic statements of the main lines or workings of
their topics and assessments of their theological impact.

Already available are *Nonfoundationalism* by John E. Thiel
and *Literary Theory* by David Dawson. Forthcoming titles
in the series include *Hermeneutics* by Francis Schüssler
Fiorenza, *Feminist Theory* by Serene Jones, *Critical Social
Theory* by Gary M. Simpson, *Theories of Culture* by Kathryn Tanner, and *Postmodernity* by Paul Lakeland.

GUIDES TO
THEOLOGICAL
INQUIRY

Literary Theory

∞

David Dawson

Fortress Press / Minneapolis

To my students
in Religion and Comparative Literature
at Haverford College, 1992 and 1994

LITERARY THEORY
Guides to Theological Inquiry series

Biblical quotations, unless otherwise noted, are from the New Revised Standard Version of the Bible, copyright © 1989 by the Division of Christian Education of the National Council of Churches of Christ in the United States of America. Used by permission.

The excerpt from "Domination of Black" by Wallace Stevens, from *The Palm at the End of the Mind: Selected Poems and a Play by Wallace Stevens*, edited by Holly Stevens (New York: Vintage Books, 1972) is copyright © 1967, 1969, 1971 by Holly Stevens and used by permission.

Cover design: Terry Bentley

Library of Congress Cataloging-in-Publication Data

Dawson, David, 1957–
    Literary theory / David Dawson.
        p.   cm.—(Guides to theological inquiry)
    Includes bibliographical references (p.   ).
    ISBN 0-8006-2693-1 (alk. paper)
        1. Criticism.   2. Religion and literature.   I. Title.
    II. Series
    PN49.D35   1995
    801'.95—dc20   95-5492
                                                                                 CIP

The paper used in this publication meets the minimum requirements of American National Standard for Information Sciences—Permanence of Paper for Printed Library Materials, ANSI Z329.48-1984.   (∞)™

Manufactured in the U.S.A.   AF 1–2693
99   98   97   96   95   1   2   3   4   5   6   7   8   9   10

Contents

Foreword

No self-sufficient enterprise, Christian theology always proceeds in intellectual dialogue with other forms of inquiry. Perhaps a habit fostered by chance in the Hellenistic milieu in which Christianity achieved its greatest initial success, perhaps a necessary outcome of its desire to speak from a Christian point of view about the whole of life—whatever the reason—theology had philosophy as its dialogue partner from the first and for much of its history. With the contraction, however, of philosophy's scope in the late nineteenth century and the parceling out of its domain to the disciplines of the modern academy (economics, politics, psychology, etc.), the theologian's task of keeping up this dialogue became more difficult. The aim of the *Guides to Theological Inquiry* series is to help ease this burden by familiarizing people with major academic movements and disciplines and by clarifying the ways in which they might be of continuing importance for theological investigation.

Arguing that literary theory is one academic discipline that has not relinquished the traditional aspirations of philosophy and theology to interpret the whole of reality, David Dawson in this volume of the series brings literary theory and theology together as equal partners in a dialogue about shared matters of human concern. The book that results from this innovative procedure of mutual interrogation and conversation between theology and literary theory offers its readers a lucid and sure-footed introduction to some of the more arcane figures of modern literary criticism—Bloom, Derrida, de Man, and Bakhtin—as well as a series of nuanced and provocative explorations of particular theological issues, organized around the topics of spirit, text, and body.

Kathryn Tanner

Acknowledgments

A t both the beginning and end of this project, student insight was the most important stimulus for my own reflection, writing, and revision. In particular, I want to express my debt to those Haverford and Bryn Mawr students who took my seminar in Contemporary Religious Thought during the period in which I was writing this book. In the Fall of 1992, students probed the texts with me as I began to put together a first draft, and their interpretations did much to shape my early efforts to think about theory theologically. The 1992 seminar included Gordon Adams, Jennifer Burch, Allison Cohen, Margaret Dunkly, Kate Felmet, Sarah Frazier, Jessica Jernigan, Erin Jospe, Gordon McClellan, Kevin McCulloch, Arielle Metz, Carrie Porter, Dan Rafferty, John Stephan, Amy Weismann, and Rachel White. A penultimate draft was tested against fresh student readings of the primary texts, this time in the Fall of 1994. The 1994 seminar members were Ted Alsedek, Amy Blau, Stephen Hock, Amanda Irwin, Anne Kenderdine, Jung Kim, Erin Langan, Catherine Partridge, Eric Rassbach, Sam Robfogel, Lila Shapiro, Lissa Weinberger, and Brooke Wells. Among those just mentioned, I must single out two persons for special mention. Kevin McCulloch and Rachel White followed the project with enthusiasm from the outset and offered especially helpful critical responses to the manuscript as it was developing.

My colleagues in Haverford's Religion Department—Seth Brody, Richard Luman, Anne McGuire, and Michael Sells—offered productive responses to my arguments as I developed them in various drafts. The theological aspects of the book were probed with characteristic intensity of analysis and generosity of spirit by members of the Yale-Washington Theology Group. The ability and willingness of the members of this group to subordinate their own agendas for the sake of understanding and improving the work of another member is unparalleled in my experience. Stephen Finley of Haverford's English Department and Carol Bernstein of Bryn Mawr's English Department found time in the midst of extraordinarily busy schedules to give the entire manuscript a much needed literary theoretical scrutiny. Many of the things I say in this book would be contested in one way or another by all of my readers, and I am grateful for the opportunity I've had to reconceive or hone my arguments in dialogue and debate with them all. Naturally, I alone am responsible for what is written here, including all of its shortcomings.

Finally, the book exists only because J. Michael West from Fortress Press and Kathryn Tanner from the University of Chicago Divinity School first enticed me to write it and then helped me to do so. I am grateful to both of them for the invitation to contribute to this series and for their warm encouragement and concrete assistance along the way. Finishing the editorial process turned out to be a surprisingly painless task, largely due to the perceptive work of copy editor Sheryl Strauss, who helped me transform what I had originally written into a more precise and readable version of what I really wanted to say.

Introduction

Christianity is a religion of conversion, or turning away from one life orientation toward another. After the turn, the convert's prior stance looks different; the convert now sees his or her past from the vantage point of his or her "new being." Both Hebrew Scripture and the cosmos as a whole (including the realms of nature, history, and culture) become subject to such a reseeing or revision in Christianity. In the rereading of Hebrew Scripture, the turn of Christian conversion takes the literary form of *trope*— a word or phrase that turns away from one meaning (often regarded as the literal meaning) toward another. Christian readers ascribe to the language of the Hebrew Bible such turnings, by which words become figures of meanings other than those that once seemed obvious. For the Christian reader, the troping of the Hebrew Bible so that it becomes the Christian Old Testament foreshadows (or, from another point of view, reflects) the reader's own turning toward the person of Christ. Although largely unconcerned with religious conversion, literary theorists Paul de Man and Harold Bloom are much concerned with the character of tropes. Their debate over the nature and function of tropes intersects in various unexpected and illuminating ways with Christian theological reflection on conversion in response to the incarnation of God in Christ.

The converted Christian's new relation to God involves interpreting all of reality as subject to that God's will. This universal interpretation generally includes some account of the ongoing relations between human self-assertion and divine agency. Here, trope may become too limited a category, one insufficiently stretched out over time—the time required for a human life (or human history) to unfold in response to various divine initiatives. So Christians, following biblical precedent, often turn to story or narrative as the literary form best suited for depicting complex human and divine actions

1

in coherent, ongoing temporal relation to one another. Although contemporary secular novels appear to depict human action independent of divine agency, such agency may be more concealed or transformed than abandoned or denied. The Russian theorist Mikhail Bakhtin locates a comparable agency in the novel's author, whose daunting task it is to bring the radically free actions of human characters to their noncoerced, unachieved, but intrinsically inevitable, consummations. Bakhtin's understanding of the finalizing or consummating author in relation to the author's would-be heroes intersects in provocative ways with classical Christian theological accounts of providential divine agency in a world of free human agents.

These intersections of poetic trope and religious conversion, novelistic narrative and divine providence, suggest the possibility of a new kind of conversation between literary theorists and Christian theologians. This new conversation would differ from one that is already well under way. For some time now, theologians have been mining modern and postmodern literary theories for up-to-date ways to interpret biblical texts. And literary theorists have increasingly paid attention to the early Jewish and Christian interpretative antecedents to their own strategies of reading. But relatively little has been done to explore how Christian theology and literary theory might be mutually stimulating at the level of the sort of ambitious, universal reflection that theology represents. This is so even though contemporary literary theorists typically display interpretative aspirations that rival those of theologians in scope; they routinely make pronouncements on, or implicitly make assumptions about, the nature of meaning, reality, and human being. Although some have recognized that contemporary literary theory often functions much like a secular version of classical theology, few have taken this claim as a serious invitation to probe literary theory precisely as a theology.

The closest that some thinkers come to making such a probe often turns into an embarrassing, adversarial encounter. Theologians and theorists can easily turn against one another, theologians lamenting the antihumanism or nihilism of postmodern theory, theorists taking the Christian theological tradition to task for a naive faith in the sacramental or incarnational presence of meaning in texts. Of course, the players can change roles: contemporary theorists can charge one another with nihilism or naiveté, and avant-garde theologians can indict the classical theological tradition for various sorts of essentializing or reifying impulses.[1] But theological charges of antihumanism or nihilism do not always reflect serious reckoning with the theoretical claim that some theologically favored constructions of "the human," when they masquerade as "the natural" or "the divinely given," have been pernicious. And literary theoretical complaints about naive incarnationalism do not always attend carefully to the subtle distinctions and qualifications made in virtually any classic Christian text that takes up the topic of divine presence. If this book does nothing else, I hope it makes these sorts of superficial judgments more difficult to make or accept.

My primary goal can be stated more positively: I want to probe ways in which literary theory might foster Christian theological insight, and ways in which theology might do the same for theory. For such a project to begin, there is no need for theorists to affirm the reality of a deity (though, of course, some do); nor must theologians give up such belief (though, of course, some have). Ever since Ludwig Feuerbach announced that theology is an inverted anthropology (God is humanity writ large), or Kenneth Burke observed that, whatever else it might be, theology is always *logology* (talk about God is always talk about language), we have had the modern starting points needed for theorists and theologians to be able to begin to talk to one another about their meanings, if not their truths.[2] Before their conversations advance too far, theologians and theorists will also need to talk about their truths if their conversations are not to remain superficial. Dealing with the particularities of theoretical and theological meanings is a necessary first step. I will remain content with meaning—at least until the Epilogue, where I venture a few tentative remarks about truth.

General Approach

The strategy of this book is to correlate close readings of theoretical and theological particularities. I ask readers to work with me at reading side by side the details of complex literary theoretical texts and equally complex Christian theological writings. The challenge here is not so much to get clear about the nuances of Christian theology (although intratheological debates about them are complex and ongoing). The real challenge is to engage the details of Christianity with those of literary theories. Literary theorists rightly complain that Christian theologians often do not attend sufficiently to particular features of culture before making a Christian assessment of them. Christians must engage culture in its own integrity if the redescription that follows conversion is not to become a simple replacement—a changing of the question. I hasten to add, however, that while theologians should not evade an issue by changing the question, both Christian theologians and literary theorists should be able to disagree over how to frame the most rewarding questions about what they nonetheless regard as matters of shared human concern.

By adopting this strategy of correlating particularities, I hope to offer readers not so much a set of probable claims as a set of possible clues— suggestions about the kinds of reflections a Christian theological engagement with literary theory might set in motion. To do this, I identify points at which the theories themselves invite a comparison with theology because of some apparent convergence of interests, and then allow theory and theology to pose questions to each other. Ideally, this interrogation will take place not at the points of maximum similarity or maximum difference alone, but rather at those doubly charged points of closest convergence and strongest divergence. My aim is to identify precisely those points of shared human concern at which the literary theorist and the Christian theologian seem very close and yet, perhaps in ways only discernible when that closeness is recognized, remain strongly opposed.

At a minimum, I want to encourage the kind of reflection in which one person can take both Christian theology and literary theory seriously enough on their own terms so that their convergences and divergences might assume humanly compelling significance. A more ambitious goal is to highlight specific points of contrast-within-similarity in order to explain why a Christian theologian might gain something theologically by reading literary theory, or why a literary theorist might want to read Christian theology in order to gain literary theoretical insight. Nevertheless, my discussion of literary theorists is framed from the perspective of a Christian theologian. An inevitable consequence of my theological focus will surely be, at least in places, to oversimplify or simply fail to grasp aspects of literature and literary theory that will strike professionals in those fields as obvious and important. I hope that such instances will be few, and that my theological perspective will help all readers understand these literary perspectives in new and illuminating ways.

This study is not a comparative analysis of methodologies. I do not try to juxtapose literary theory with theological method—even though academic theology turned into theological method at about the same time that practical literary criticism turned into literary theory, and perhaps for much the same reason—as an apologetic or protectionist strategy by humanists who found themselves increasingly marginalized by the rising prestige of science and technology in the university. The most stimulating contemporary literary theories, including those considered in this book, self-consciously present themselves as nontheoretical. They resist the notion that they constitute independent bodies of general conceptual formulations with quasi-predictive or regulative goals, and they deny themselves the dubious status of independent self-reflections on their own proper manner of formulation. Instead, they offer inductive generalizations that are both based on, and designed to take their readers back to, a direct engagement with literature. Harold Bloom wants to bring before us the revisionary dynamics of poetic creativity; Paul de Man wants to bring us to a lucid recognition of the fundamentally linguistic character of literature; Mikhail Bakhtin wants us to see how a successful novelist crafts a verbal environment in which characters realize themselves through the consummating and embodying visions of their authors. So I will regard Christian theology and literary theory as reflections on direct and ongoing encounters with their respective objects of attention: God (as believed in and represented by the Christian community) and literature (as produced by its authors and received by its readers). In the epilogue, I will consider the extent to which both literary theory and Christian theology, as second-order reflective activities, are finally justified by their ability to take their users back to enhanced first-order encounters with their objects of attention.

The remainder of the introduction addresses the method and argument of this study and discusses its larger theological rationale. The method involves appealing to three central categories (spirit, text, body) as bridges on which literary theorists and Christian theologians might meet for debate. The argument concerns how the literary theories of Harold Bloom, Paul de Man, and Mikhail Bakhtin converge toward, or diverge from, the classical Christian understanding of divine incarnation.[3] The introduction concludes with a discussion of the project's larger theological rationale and considers some possible objections to it. That rationale is rooted in the classical Christian aspiration to give a Christian construal of everything we call reality; the objections concern such an aspiration's totalizing and overgeneralizing potential.

Method and Argument

To have a genuine debate, speakers must believe that they are, in some sense, talking about a common topic, or talking to one another while standing on common ground. One cannot say in advance what sort of thing that topic or ground must be, or what sort of description would be most adequate to it. But at some level, interlocutors must sense that they share something, if only because they find themselves wanting to talk to one another. The debate in this book takes place on a common ground marked out by the categories of *spirit, text,* and *body.* These categories are bridges on which Christian theologians and literary theorists might encounter one another. Like real bridges, these conceptual bridges are meant to be functional, without content or meaning in their own right (the analogy soon breaks down, of course, since real-life bridges, as architectural objects, have an aesthetic dimension apart from their function). By calling them bridges, I intentionally avoid calling them mediating concepts: they are intended to open up a space or opportunity for an encounter, but not all encounters can or should be mediated. For example, *text* marks a site where Christian reflection about Scripture and literary theoretical discussion of textuality might encounter one another. But this is not meant to imply, in advance of actual analysis, that Christians regard their Scripture as an instance of textuality, or that literary theorists treat their examples of textuality as scripture. My use of the categories of spirit, text, and body is not intended to trade secretly on, or to privilege, specifically theological or literary usages, but only to give those usages a place to meet. As empty placeholders for which the relevant specifying and concretizing content will need to be supplied by actual theological and theoretical usages of language, the three bridge categories are intended to make it possible for theologians and theorists to meet one another in their own particularity and individuality. These categories make such meetings possible because they point toward essential features of both Christian self-identity and contemporary literary theory.

Body, Spirit, and Text in Christian Theology

Body, spirit, and text point toward crucial aspects of the central moment in the Christian account of reality, the incarnation of the Word (*logos*) of God (or Son of God) in Jesus of Nazareth and the appropriation of that event by the church. The category of *body* makes a place for the church's proclamation that God in the person of the Word became incarnate in Jesus of Nazareth, who was himself a fully embodied person—a human being who lacked no dimension of human personhood, least of all a body capable of dying. According to the traditional teaching of most Christian churches, Jesus was regarded by his Jewish followers as the promised Messiah (in Greek, *Christos* or "anointed one") who would soon lead the people of Israel to victory over their oppressors. The unexpected death of Jesus made his followers skeptical about his messianic status. But the seemingly invalidated Messiah was surprisingly validated by God, a validation to which the resurrection narratives of the Gospels give testimony. The category of *spirit* opens up a place for the action of God in the person of the Holy Spirit upon the inner lives or human spirits of Jesus' followers. They announced that the Holy Spirit had made present to them the risen, embodied Jesus. The category of *text* points toward another key feature of the founding event of Christianity: the production of Scripture and other writings. Through their experience of the risen (and still embodied) Jesus, the disciples were led to interpret existing Scripture (the Hebrew Bible) as the Christian Old Testament and to compose new Scripture (the New Testament), as well as other kinds of Christian literature.

The turning point in the event of incarnation was the surprising reversal of Jesus' status from crucified to resurrected Messiah. This reversal has been understood in at least three very different ways, which can be called classical Christian, Christian revisionist, and radical revisionist. The classical Christian understanding locates the reversal of the crucified Messiah's status in God's resurrection of him from the dead, which overcame the disenchantment of his disciples. The Holy Spirit, making present the resurrected Jesus to his followers, enabled them to reread Hebrew Scripture and thereby discover that the Messiah's unexpected death had in fact been prophesied. They then created Christian Scripture in order to give written representation to their present spiritual experience of Jesus as the risen Christ, describing the career of Jesus as the fulfillment of Hebrew prophecy.

Christian revisionist accounts, such as Rudolf Bultmann's, focus on the disciples' experience of the spiritual presence of the crucified Jesus rather than on a divine act of resurrection.[4] In the wake of Jesus' death but with an inner sense of his continuing, postcrucifixion spiritual presence, Jesus' followers reread Hebrew Scripture and discovered that, contrary to their earlier understanding, the Messiah had come precisely in order to die. Because they were convinced that, despite his death, he still lived spiritually in their hearts, they composed gospels that interpreted Jesus' precrucifixion life in light of his continuing postcrucifixion presence, an "Easter faith" or "Christ experience" to which they gave symbolic expression by composing resurrection narratives.

Finally, from the deist Hermann Reimarus in the eighteenth century to Frank Kermode in the late twentieth, radical revisionist accounts have also been made of the reversal of Jesus' status, framed from a perspective that philosopher Paul Ricoeur has called the "hermeneutics of suspicion."[5] Such accounts often begin with human disenchantment rather than with either a divine resurrection of a dead Jesus or the miraculous rise of an "Easter faith." According to this radical interpretation, Jesus' followers, forced to justify their now disconfirmed faith in a Messiah as conquering king, reread Hebrew Scripture in order to prove (perhaps first of all to themselves) that, contrary to popular expectation, the Messiah had come precisely in order to die. They then composed gospels that, in effect, cast the results of that rereading into realistic, historylike biographies of Jesus. On this view, the results of a nonliteral reading of one text (Hebrew Scripture) take the form of literal representations in another (the New Testament depiction of the person and career of Jesus, including the representation of his ultimate significance by means of resurrection narratives).

This book presupposes the classical Christian account, but some readers may prefer the Christian revisionist version, others the radical revisionist version. I sketch out these options only to suggest that regardless of the account one prefers, virtually any formulation that takes seriously the basic (and divergent) testimonies of Christian tradition will find the categories of spirit, text, and body centrally important. However interpreted, those categories gesture toward the central features of the event called incarnation, as that event took root in the Christian imagination.

The Christian community that emerged in response to that event continues to invoke realities marked by text, body, and spirit as it relates the Old and New Testaments to each other, to the embodied person of Jesus, and to the Holy Spirit that animates all proper interpretation. The community's principal ongoing engagement with the past event of incarnation takes place in the Eucharist or Lord's Supper. This sacrament brings together spirit (as the Holy Spirit makes present to the communicant's human spirit the risen, embodied Christ), body (as the elements of bread and wine become or otherwise reveal the resurrected body of Christ), and text (as the words of institution spoken in the eucharistic liturgy unite the spiritual presence of the risen Christ with all of Scripture, christologically understood). Filled with the Holy Spirit making present the risen Christ whose character and identity are depicted by Scripture, the community regards itself as the body of Christ. By participation in the Eucharist, members of the community are led to relate to one another and to their divine creator through the same disposition of self-giving love according to which all of reality was created, redeemed, and will ultimately be fulfilled.

Spirit, Text, and Body in Literary Theory

We have seen how spirit, text, and body might provide placeholders for important aspects of the central event of Christian self-definition. These categories also point toward three influential tendencies in contemporary literary theory: a defense of the human spirit or subject via a celebration of poetic imagination and creativity; an emphasis on textuality or linguistic rhetoricity that seemingly dissolves human beings as subjects of their experiences or agents of their acts; and more recent efforts to make the human body an inescapable feature of the production, circulation, and reception of literary discourse.

The work of Harold Bloom represents the continuing force in contemporary literary theoretical reflection of neo-Romantic appeals to the human spirit as imaginative, original, and creative. From his early studies of English (and later, American) Romantic poets in the late 1950s through the 1960s, to his development of a theory of poetic influence in the 1970s and 1980s, up to his more recent discussions of the Bible, William Shakespeare, Sigmund Freud, and the "American Religion," Bloom has continued to reinvoke, while radically revising, the irreducibly experiential basis of both poetic creation and practical criticism. At the center of Bloom's poetic theory is his characterization of poetic creation as an *agon* or struggle between a new, would-be poet (or "ephebe," from the Greek for "young man") and his poetic precursor—the strong poetic predecessor whom the ephebe loves but, in the process of trying to escape his or her suffocating influence, also comes to hate. Bloom's numerous writings chart the labyrinthine ways by which the ephebe strives to overcome his sense of belatedness and futility, his recognition that there is now nothing left to write because prior great poets seemingly have said it all—and said it definitively.

To become a poet in his own right while viewing himself at the end of a formidable poetic tradition, the ephebe must become a "strong reader" of his precursor's poetry. He does this by composing his own poems in ways that "trope" the precursor's work by simultaneously embracing and revising the central patterns of imagery and argument in the precursor's poem. If successful (and no poet—with the possible exceptions of J or the Yahwist, author of a major strand of the Hebrew Bible, and Shakespeare—is more than partially successful), the ephebe creates a new poem that strikes readers as the original of which the precursor's poem is but a deficient and highly derivative copy. In Bloom's hands, a poem's allusions to prior poems, which an earlier generation of critics regarded as evidence of benign and generous literary influence, become the strange and various "dialectics," "ratios," and "defenses" of the new, would-be poet. Oedipus-like, the ephebe figuratively slays his strong poetic father in order to carve out imaginative space for his own original poem. The category of spirit points toward the dark and dynamic inner impulse that Bloom identifies as the motive force for all strong (that is, revisionary) poetry.

Harold Bloom is an astoundingly prolific author, and no brief study can do more than begin to reckon with his works' vast scope, intertextual complexity, and arcane terminology. In my discussion, I focus attention on the central, early theoretical statement, *The Anxiety of Influence,* with help from a number of other works, especially *A Map of Misreading* and the concluding methodological "Coda" to *Wallace Stevens: The Poems of Our Climate.*[6] Bloom's already long and rich career is still unfolding (or, better, exfoliating): books, lectures, and reviews continue to pour forth, as though he were intent on enacting the unfinalizable character of orality by textual means.[7] Bloom's defense of an inalienable human subjectivity by means of his own baroque rhetorical performance bears witness to the persistence of a chastened, ever-darkening, neo-Romantic spirit in the midst of a poststructuralist linguistic determinism that would seem to dissolve all such spirit into pure textuality.

Another, very different strand of neo-Romantic theorizing has emerged in the wake of structuralism and poststructuralism. Both movements repudiate Romanticism's expressive view of language and hermeneutical view of interpretation. Following Ferdinand de Saussure, structural linguistics sets aside language as referential expression (*parole*) in order to study language as a self-contained system (*langue*).[8] Poststructuralism focuses on the "play of signifiers"—the way signifiers are not only set free from reference to the world, but also from any literary system or structure that might seek to contain or control them by giving them determinate meanings. Paul de Man represents the literary theoretical application of that form of post-structuralist theory (or reading technique) known as deconstruction. Like Bloom, de Man is a shrewd reader and defender of Romantic literature, and he presents his theory as a description of the inherent linguistic workings of the language of that literature.

Despite the sheer density and conceptual rigor of de Man's writings, most readers are likely to find de Man easier to read than Bloom. Much less poetically resonant and allusive than Bloom's, de Man's prose typically consists of rather straightforward, analytical argument. I will focus on three essays in particular: the early "Rhetoric of Temporality" and the later essays "Rhetoric of Persuasion (Nietzsche)" and "Shelley Disfigured."[9] These three essays reveal an increasing elaboration of de Man's theory and practice of deconstructive reading. In the first essay, de Man's reading reveals the way the linguistic character of language undermines its apparent offer of meaning; the essay on Friedrich Nietzsche complicates this picture of language's power of internal subversion, charting a constant, unresolved oscillation between language's claim to assert truth and its apparent performative power to enact a deed. The late essay on Percy Bysshe Shelley focuses on the violent, coercive workings of that performative or "positing" power of language in its own right. Taken together as a series, the essays outline an increasingly severe view of language: as failed effort at knowledge; as undecidable oscillation between knowledge and performance; as arbitrary and violent imposition of power.

De Man's career began and continued in relative obscurity for many years, though his single-minded commitment to literary theory as a rigorous, near-scientific analysis of the actual functioning of literary language gained him a coterie of students of rare intelligence, devotion, and respect. His writings gained a significant critical audience only in the late 1960s, but his influence surged in the 1970s, only to be abruptly cut off at its height by his unexpected death in 1983.[10] The theorist and his writings were soon embroiled in controversy when it was discovered that the youthful de Man had written reviews for a collaborationist newspaper in wartime Belgium, reviews that in several places appear to express anti-Semitic sentiments. The resulting arguments about de Man's early wartime journalism have been heated and ongoing, and that subject will not be part of my direct discussion of de Man in this book. I will note in passing, however, some possible connections between de Man's theorizing and his apparent reluctance to acknowledge his morally problematic past. His theory does seem to render difficult any conception of a subject or self sufficiently self-continuous to be capable of retrospective moral self-assessment.

In addition to their continuing direct influence, the theories of Bloom and de Man also indirectly inform a variety of contemporary literary theoretical perspectives. Culture studies, film theory, gender studies, performance theory, New Historicism, and neocolonial theory are some recent influences on literary theory (or, in some cases, versions of literary theory) that have either assimilated or rejected a variety of Bloom's and de Man's insights. In addition, the principal struggle represented by my discussion of Bloom and de Man—between a defense of a human subject irreducible to textuality and a construal of all reality (including human subjects) as modes of textuality—remains central to many current literary theoretical (as well as Christian theological) debates.

One important way that current debate has shifted since the earlier exchanges between Bloom and de Man has been to redirect talk about the "subject," away from experiential and textual categories, toward the category of the body. The subject in contemporary literary theory is increasingly seen as inevitably situated because necessarily embodied (and hence gendered, encultured, and politicized). The work of the Russian thinker Mikhail Bakhtin represents recent efforts to make "the body" central for literary theoretical reflection. Although Bakhtin is an elder contemporary of Bloom and de Man, his influence on literary theory is more recent than theirs, due to the early suppression of his works in the former Soviet Union and their delayed translation into English. Bakhtin's notions of carnival and carnivalization have been especially significant for recent literary theory. But the Bakhtin I find most promising for dialogue between literary theory and Christian theology is the author of the early, recently translated, and still largely unfamiliar essays "Author and Hero in Aesthetic Activity" and *Toward a Philosophy of the Act.*[11] In these works, Bakhtin represents otherness, not as unavoidable antagonist or semantic absence, but as a necessary enabling condition for the authorship of novelistic characters, as well as for all genuine human flourishing.

I chose these particular theorists for two basic reasons. First, each in his own way represents an important impulse in contemporary literary theory: one can map a great deal of current controversy among literary theorists by asking whether a theorist wishes to defend some form of human experience or subjecthood irreducible to textuality, some form of textual constitution of self and world, or some form of the body as the inescapable starting point for literary reflection. Although the diversity and complexity of the current literary theoretical scene cannot be comprehensively represented by any three figures, close attention to the leading concerns of these theorists can provide insight into some of the deepest motivations of contemporary literary theory, even when it circulates under other rubrics or is associated with other thinkers. My second reason for selecting Bloom, de Man, and Bakhtin is that they have stimulated me to develop the particular claims about the relations between literary theory and Christian theology that I want to advance in this book. Consequently, my selection represents a compromise between a desire to offer theological readers a reasonable and not-too-idiosyncratic introduction to some representative impulses in contemporary literary theory, and a desire to advance my own particular argument.

That argument consists of a set of interrelated claims, which readers are invited to assess in light of their own reflection on the primary texts I consider. Viewed from the standpoint of Christian theology, the literary theories of Harold Bloom and Paul de Man mark out anti-incarnational extremes of hyperspritualism and hypertextuality. Reinterpreting the Romantic heritage that he advances through both radical revision and resistance, Bloom reduces the motive force of poetry to the power of a disembodied, agonistic human spark or *pneuma* (spirit), which, despite Bloom's occasional disavowals, defines for him "the essentially human." De Man, also revising received views of Romanticism by pushing in poststructuralist directions some of the insights of existentialism, New Criticism, and structuralism, attacks what might be regarded as literary forms of sacramental grace, construes all instances of "the literary" as a hyperliteralistic textuality, and seemingly dissolves the human self as a nontextual reality in the process. Consequently, while Bloom gives us disembodiment of self and meaning into spirit, de Man offers a hyperkenosis (or complete emptying out) of self and meaning into letter. Both the hyperspiritualist and hypertextualist extremes are forced to reckon with each other, however. For de Man, the extremes endlessly converge only to diverge, producing the undecidable oscillation between language as performance and language as assertion that he calls an *aporia*. For Bloom, the extremes converge at the site of a relentless psychological and linguistic struggle between precursor and ephebe, and Bloom grudgingly celebrates the grim glory of that all-too-human battle, in opposition to what he regards as the antihumanistic bleakness of de Man's alternative. Not surprisingly, Bloom and de Man turn out to be each other's most menacing "other."

These two anti-incarnationalist theories involve highly sublimated aspects of Christianity's relation to Judaism. Bloom's hyperspirituality explicitly rejects the incarnational claims of traditional Christianity, and along with it, orthodox Judaism's interpretation of Torah, which also insists that the divine intention is realized in the flesh. With respect to Christianity, Bloom simultaneously criticizes Christian revisionary reading of Hebrew Scripture while evading traditional Christianity's insistence that, however revisionary it may be, it is intrinsically related to Judaism. De Man makes assumptions about language and meaning (in order to undermine them) that echo assumptions made by some Christian revisionsts such as Marcion who themselves were hostile to Christianity's relation to Judaism. Although de Man tries to undermine these views of language and meaning, his sub-version is simply an inversion that trades on shared assumptions.

Finally, I examine the violence that seems to haunt both theorists: the violence of the ephebe's struggle with precursors and the violence of the positing power of language. The strength of these visions lies in their recognition of what Christian theologians would call sin: the desperate struggle of Bloom's ephebe for originality is, as Bloom in his celebration of John Milton's Satan as archetypal modern poet acknowledges, a version of Adam's claim of God's autonomy for himself. Likewise, the coercive hegemony of the textuality that de Man's reading exposes looks like a postmodern instance of ancient Greek and Roman notions of fate, astral determinism, or sheer chance. Because they deny God's providential agency over the divinely created order of things, fate, astral determinism, and chance have often been regarded by Christians as worldviews consistent with Adam's presumptuous claim.

The violence to which these theorists point, though it can be interpreted religiously as manifestation of sin, is rooted theoretically in the theorists' commitment to an essentially monistic conception of reality. In these two monistic visions, difference or otherness can only be regarded as fundamentally at odds with primal unity, as fundamentally adversarial or mutually destructive. The monism of both theories clashes head-on with Christianity, which proclaims neither a monistic nor a dualistic view of things but rather a complex, paradoxical difference-within-unity in which differences turn out to be the necessary means to the self-constitution of the integrity of the whole. Christian opposition to both monism and dualism is grounded in the doctrine of a triune deity, a deity that creates a reality other than itself for the purpose of a fuller expression of that love that its own self-differentiation expresses. In contrast to Bloom's and de Man's visions, in the Christian view of things the only reason for "the other" is the expression of love.

Mikhail Bakhtin offers a perspective that acknowledges and embraces features of late nineteenth- and early twentieth-century Russian literary theory similar in crucial respects to those advanced later in the West by Bloom and de Man. But Bakhtin privileges neither spirit nor text but the human body; as a result, the incarnational sensibility of classical Christian theology seems to find a correlate in Bakhtin's starting point of embodiment. But Bakhtin's perspective may not be without its own theological problems. His celebration of an aesthetic perspective not only seems to neglect de Man's warning about the perennial human attraction of self-mystifying (and self-serving) wholes, but also to disregard Bloom's recognition of the reality of interpersonal malevolence. Although Bakhtin's perspective may initially strike Christian theologians as considerably more congenial than either Bloom's or de Man's, a warning is in order: Theologians will need to assess carefully the temptation Bakhtin's theory offers—a temptation to underestimate the presence of evil and to overestimate the value of unity.

Bakhtin's celebration of consummation and wholeness reflects the essentially comedic character of the Christian vision, in marked contrast to Bloom's tragic vision and de Man's neo-Stoicism. But Bakhtin may gain this comedic character at the cost of an incipient monism of his own, despite his insistence on the centrality of otherness and dialogue. Ironically, the apparent absence in Bakhtin's vision of a genuinely malevolent other calls into question the seriousness of his category of otherness: do those whose primary role consists in the completion of one another's lack have sufficient weight to be "others"—genuinely autonomous selves—in their own right? In the Christian account of things, unless an "other" has a will truly independent of one's own and of the deity's, he or she is not really an other at all. One telltale sign of the genuineness of a will sufficiently free to respond in love to divine love lies in one's ability to turn that will against others or against the deity. Only such a radically adversarial possibility could justify the radical self-othering or *kenōsis* of God called for by classic Christian conceptions of redemption. Such a radical self-othering on God's part would be the deepest expression of that love for which a truly free other was necessary, and for which a truly malevolent other was at least possible if not inevitable. I will argue that Bakhtin can be read as making room for this possibility, but doing so requires that one pay close attention to the lines that he draws between aesthetics and ethics.

Rationale and Objections

This book is intended primarily for Christian theologians and other students of Christian thought, but I hope that literary theorists will be able to profit from it as well. There is a clear reason for even the most atheological of literary theorists to pay attention to Christian theology, grounded in theory's own unquestioned assumption of the human significance (apart from the truth or desirability) of all cultural constructions, including theology. This assumption remains in place even for those literary theorists who are inclined to smoke out and attack sublimations of the theological in various representations of the human or conceptions of humanism—at least as long as they continue to write and publish as though it mattered whether what they wrote were ever read by other human beings.

The specifically Christian theological rationale for attending to literary theory on its own terms is grounded in Christianity's self-conception. Classical Christian theology has often defined itself as "faith seeking understanding." "Faith" denotes an ensemble of distinctive beliefs, dispositions, and practices that make up individual and communal Christian life. In theology, this ensemble becomes the object of a disciplined reflection that seeks to understand it in relation to God. Its relation to God leads Christian self-understanding to range far beyond the immediate confines of any specific Christian community, however. Because the Christian perspective, though immediately rooted in concrete historical communities, strives to be universal in scope, the understanding sought by faith is equally universal, seeking to embrace and interpret everything called reality. Christian theologians justify their aspiration to interpret all of reality according to Christian categories by appealing to the doctrines of creation, incarnation, and consummation (classically summarized in the Apostles' Creed). These doctrines, working together with the Bible and the traditions that give them content and character, encompass all of reality within a single, overarching story, interpreting from a Christian point of view all that was, is, and will be.

The Christian doctrine of creation *ex nihilo* proclaims that no dimension of reality can exist that does not have a place within the divinely created order. This doctrine asserts that there is God, God's creation, and nothing else. Further, following the Johannine declaration that "all things came into being through him [the *logos*]" (John 1:3), Christians also insist that creation takes place through the same divine *logos*, which, as second person of the triune deity, subsequently became incarnate as the human being Jesus of Nazareth. As a consequence, all aspects of reality bear some relation both to the Christian triune deity and to the fully divine and fully human Jesus of Nazareth. And all aspects of reality will be brought to their fulfillment in the wake of Christ's second appearance, which will usher in a final consummation of the entire created order. This universal aspiration of Christian interpretation has been expressed in various ways. Athanasius, the ancient Greek-speaking theologian and bishop of Alexandria, observed that God's act of creation left "nothing void of his own divinity."[12] Echoing the link between incarnation and creation drawn in the prologue to John's Gospel, Augustine, Latin-speaking theologian and bishop of Hippo, declared that the *logos* "came to a place where He was already, for He was in the world, and the world was made by Him."[13] The contemporary Roman Catholic theologian Karl Rahner insisted that "every real intervention of God in his world, although it is free and cannot be deduced, is always only the becoming historical and becoming concrete of that 'intervention' in which God as the transcendental ground of the world has from the outset embedded himself in this world as its self-communicating ground."[14]

Together, then, the doctrines of creation, incarnation, and consummation provide the rationale for the thoroughgoing Christian understanding of all of reality. Given the universal scope of Christian interpretation, there can be no cultural or intellectual activity devoid of theological import. This, finally, is the principal theological reason why Christian theologians must engage literary theory. Such engagement is required regardless of the methods or self-conceptions of literary theorists, or whether they approve of the activity. What literary theorists do is simply one more aspect of that complex human culture that theologians aspire to interpret Christianly. This aspiration is prior to all debates about whether or not, or to what extent and in what manner, Christian theologians should make arguments to justify their interpretations to non-Christians. In other words, neither an apologetic, nonapologetic, or ad hoc apologetic Christian stance alters the basic universal aspirations described above; these stances are assumed from within that universal mandate.[15] Similarly, although literary theorists typically reject the charge that they are imposing global categories, their actual treatment of literature and its reading gives it a comprehensive significance—the sweep of a full-fledged worldview. Literary theoretical remarks about literature turn out, upon examination, to entail sweeping proposals about the character of reality and the place of human beings within it.

From a Christian theological standpoint, the mandate for universal interpretation stems from the doctrines of creation and consummation; the particularities of a Christian interpretative scheme stem from the doctrine of incarnation. But this is to put the matter in far too schematic a fashion. Because the God who is self-particularized in incarnation is also the creator God, and because divine self-particularization does not add to or distort but simply reveals the divine character as such, creation itself is particularized as well. That is, there is no creation in general, but only this particular creation. Consequently, for Christian reflection no universals exist that have not been particularized in a creative act that is, due to the trinitarian character of the Christian God, necessarily christological. Consequently, Christian theologians are committed to offering particular descriptions of universal scope and import.

The ultimate seriousness of a theologian's engagement with literary theory or other cultural formation is perhaps best measured by the extent to which the theologian conceives of those formations as being able in principle to alter his or her own interpretative paradigms in specific ways. Should this happen, it need not mean that the theologian has "sold out" (though it might); it might just as easily mean that he or she is giving testimony to the religious dimension of the divinely created order of things. Those who instinctively take a dim view of this stance might wish to keep in mind some words of Karl Barth, a modern Christian theologian who strongly emphasized the contrast between Christ and culture but refused to separate them:

> We can meet God only within the bounds of the human which he has determined. But just within these bounds we may meet him. He does not

spurn what is human. Quite the contrary. This is what we have to hold on to.

But human distinction goes still further. It extends to the special human activity which comes from that endowment, to what is usually called human *culture* in its higher as well as its lower branches. We all participate in it, whether as producers or as consumers, in any case as having responsibility for it. . . . God as *humanity's* Creator and Lord is still at liberty on occasion to make of human activity and its results, in spite of their problematic character, *parables* of his own eternally good willing and doing, in face of which there could be no place for any arrogant abstinence, but for reverence, joy and gratitude.[16]

No doubt Christian theologians will need to attend carefully to the import of such qualifying phrases as "which he has determined" and "problematic character." But theological descriptions of culture that lack this depth of cultural commitment or retreat from culture in "arrogant abstinence" ought to be rejected by Christian theologians for failing to take seriously the Christian insistence on the particular incarnation in human history and culture of the creating and consummating God. Taking those implications seriously means opening up theological conceptions to potential revision. Only then will such theologians deserve Barth's commendation of those Christians who truly grasp the character of a divine justice rooted not in principles but in persons:

Their concern is with humanity. From the very start they are "humanists." They are not interested in any cause as such. In regard to every cause, they simply look and ask whether and how far it will relatively and provisionally serve or hurt the cause of human beings and their right and worth. No idea, no principle, no traditional or newly established institution or organization, no old or new form of economy, state, or culture, no so-called patrimony, no prevailing habit, custom, or moral system, no ideal of education and upbringing, no form of the church, can be for them the *a priori* of what they think and speak and will, nor can any negation or contesting of certain other ideas and the social constructs corresponding to them. Their *a priori* is not a cause, however great, necessary, or splendid it may appear to be or is. It is the righteousness of God in Jesus Christ and therefore, in correspondence with this, the human persons who are loved by God, their right and worth—solely and simply them.[17]

The doctrines of creation, incarnation, and consummation outlined above give one reason to regard the objects of theoretical and theological reflection as potentially the same at some hypothetical basic level of what is humanly experienced. I use the term *hypothetical* to indicate that I do not want to appeal to some theory or assumption about a prelinguistic or prethematic dimension of experience. I am persuaded that what is experienced is always experienced in some way or other, according to conceptual, cultural, and linguistic schemes already in place, and that the ways of perceiving provided by literary theories and Christian theologies are not the same. In general, it is a mistake to point to similarities too quickly, for even when interpretative schemes appear to be saying the same thing, one can reasonably be suspicious that on some level they are not. To say that interpretative schemes differ, however, is no justification for concluding that the functions they perform as interpretations are entirely different. It is a profound theological error—at least from the Christian perspective I have outlined above—to grant to humanly perceptible difference an ontological privilege deeper than that which we are willing to grant to humanly perceived similarity. If the word *hypothetical* does not quite make my point, perhaps *asymptotic* is better. I want to take my juxtapositions of literary theory and Christian theology as far in the direction of possible convergence on shared matters of human experience as I can, without positing as the basis for any possible convergence some theory about their necessary identity.

Among many possible objections to the universal aspiration of Christian theology, two require brief comment. Some may object that the universal claim is a pretension to cultural hegemony that, even if once accepted by "Christendom" as a goal (or a given), should now, in the light of our radically pluralistic cultures, no longer be recognized. Theologians might respond by arguing that worry about the possible negative consequences of making claims for universal import does not by itself address the theological assertion that such claims are intrinsic to Christianity. At best (this response might continue), such worry provides good reason for ameliorating the possible bad effects of the claims in some way. (Postmodernists who protest against universal claims should read again Nietzsche's stern warning against the perennial, self-deluding temptation to reject precisely those truths one hates; presumably this advice does not change when the truths one does not hate happen to be Nietzschean.)

A second response to this objection might be that claims for universality need not necessarily turn into sheer totalizing hegemony as long as the door can swing both ways. Such a response can take several forms. The first and strongest form insists that as long as Christians care at least as much about whether their interpretations of reality are humanly adequate and life-enhancing as they do about whether they are sufficiently "Christian" as measured by some existing canonical norm, there is no item of non-Christian insight that should not in principle be capable of falsifying a Christian interpretation of things. Christians who make this response might defend it by appealing to traditional Christian notions like the oneness of the created order, the freedom of God, and the limitations (even apart from sinfulness)

of human beings. Of course, Christian conceptions of what is life-enhancing or humanly adequate could never be neutral, standing altogether outside the Christian interpretative scheme. But that scheme leaves many areas
of life relatively undetermined, and Christians might well choose to interpret them in dialogue with other, non-Christian or secular conversation
partners. In any case, a strong response along such lines might agree with
Nietzsche's view that Christianity's desire for truth can (Nietzsche went
further and claimed that it not only could, but did) turn against itself,
rendering Christianity a kind of self-consuming artifact.

Those who instinctively reject this strong response out of hand run the
risk of letting their anxiety about a refutation of Christian truth lead them
to elevate selected Christian beliefs into virtual idols. For example, such
anxious Christians might hold a belief in the utter certainty of some characterization of divine revelation in such a way that they end up undermining
any meaningful belief in the freedom of God. On the other hand, those who
hold too firmly to this strong response also run the risk of idolatry, but in a
different way: they can end up turning the very principle of possible Christian capitulation into another sort of idol—one that represents an absolutiz-
ing of the characterization of Christian faith as inherently and continuously
precarious. One can become a grim but supremely self-satisfied martyr to
one's sense of inner fortitude or "courage to be."

A better response might be to grant the basic general Christian claims
about creation, human sin, divine freedom, and divine reliability, and then
to see how the specific debates between non-Christians and Christians happen to turn out. Maybe some Christian claims will need to be set aside, but
maybe not: one just waits to see where an actual debate might lead. This
response recognizes that most non-Christian challenges to Christian belief
rarely achieve sufficient depth or persuasiveness simply to knock down vital
Christian claims, which avoid capitulation by regularly adjusting themselves to meet such challenges.

One can make this second, recommended response on two somewhat
different grounds. One might do so because one simply suspects that, on
any given occasion, one might be convinced to drop particular Christian
beliefs in reponse to particular non-Christian arguments. This response
allows the Christian to join non-Christian interlocutors on common ground
(assuming, of course, that non-Christians also think that Christian challenges might force them to give up their own non-Christian beliefs). Here
one also runs the risk of sliding into the declaration that Christian capitulation must as a matter of principle be possible (and into the further risks of
either an idolatrizing remedy for, or an idolatrizing celebration of, the anxiety that such declaration might foster).

On the other hand, one might make the recommended response on the grounds that, for those with Christian faith, Christian claims are necessarily true, and therefore, whatever adjustments might be made in response to non-Christian challenges are merely different ways of expressing the truth of Christian claims, rather than actual alterations of such truth. This stance testifies to Christian confidence and assurance, though not without some risk of sliding into a non-anxiety-induced idolatry, in which a discrimination between what one happens to believe with all one's heart and what God has or has not actually done becomes increasingly hard to make.

A second objection to the universal aspiration of Christian interpretation is this: that any actual effort to develop a universal perspective (from ancient Christian *logos* theology, to Enlightenment deism, to contemporary foundational appeals to a general hermeneutics) tends to reduce the specificity of Christian beliefs to more general, more widely intelligible but less faithful notions of truth and meaningfulness. In response, theologians might argue that while things might turn out (indeed, often have turned out) this way, they need not. Although one could try to articulate a universal interpretation by means of a reduction of particulars to generalities, one might instead seek out universal import through a close reading of cultural items, both general and specific, alongside a similar reading of Christian particularities. The result would be the sort of ad hoc correlation this book attempts, a correlation unjustified by any overarching, general principles or criteria for integration or mediation, and having only as much value as is warranted by whatever insights happen to emerge.[18]

1

Spirit and Revision

Near the end of the Gospel of Luke, the resurrected Jesus encounters two of his disciples on their way to the village of Emmaus. In response to the disciples' account of the recent events in Jerusalem, the as-yet-unrecognized Jesus declares: "Oh, how foolish you are, and how slow of heart to believe all that the prophets have declared! Was it not necessary that the Messiah should suffer these things and then enter into his glory?" "Then," the gospel writer continues, "beginning with Moses and all the prophets, he interpreted to them the things about himself in all the scriptures" (Luke 24:25-27). Later, after a meal outside the village, the disciples ponder their strange, revelatory experience of Jesus' continuing presence and his interpretation of Scripture: "When he was at table with them, he took bread, blessed and broke it, and gave it to them. Then their eyes were opened, and they recognized him; and he vanished from their sight. They said to each other, 'Were not our hearts burning within us while he was talking to us on the road, while he was opening the scripture to us?'" (Luke 24:30-32).

As this gospel story indicates, conversion to Christianity was generally accompanied by a new reading of Hebrew Scripture, a revisionary reading by means of which those Jews who became Christians (and those Gentiles who followed their lead) found meanings in traditional Jewish Scripture that seemed to them to attain their deepest reality or receive their fitting fulfillment in the figure of Jesus of Nazareth. We have already observed how such revisionary reading was a troping of Hebrew Scripture, turning its apparent meanings in new, unexpected directions. This chapter examines the different understandings of tropes offered by Harold Bloom and Paul de Man in relation to the troping that occurs in Christian interpretation.

Like Christian modes of interpretation of Scripture such as typology or allegory, the literary theories of Bloom and de Man offer accounts of the literary results of reading experiences. The distinction between the literary results of reading and the reading experiences from which those results flow reminds one not to assume that similar literary forms necessarily arise from similar experiences. Although the literary results of reading described by Bloom and de Man resemble in certain ways the literary results of Christian revisionary reading, the reading experiences are fundamentally different. Christian revisionary reading can be partially understood according to literary categories such as narrative, metaphor, or metonymy, but its full character cannot be grasped without attending to the experience of faith that motivates it. Christian revisionary reading flows out of a reader's transformed relation to a God of promise and fulfillment; the literary features of the resulting interpretations are secondary to that originating experience—which is not to say that the experience is not itself deeply shaped by preexisting literary patterns. But "standing on the promises of God" is not the same thing as striving to become one's own God or fleeing from all idols, and the revisionary reading strategies these different stances generate are fundamentally different, even though they often share many literary techniques.

In the first part of this chapter, I describe two models for thinking about revisionary reading and the experiences that generate it. The first model, advanced by the structural linguist Roman Jakobson and embraced in various forms by poststructuralist literary theory, is a model of language itself. Jakobson argues that language users perform two basic tasks: they select linguistic items from a list of alternatives (the metaphoric function), and they combine their selections into meaningful syntactical units (the metonymic function).[1] The second model, well known to Christian theologians, is a model of Christian interpretation of Hebrew Scripture. Historical theologian James Preus discovers in Christian Old Testament interpretation from Augustine to Martin Luther two basic perspectives: a shadow-reality perspective, in which items in Hebrew Scripture are regarded as mere shadows of realities more fully described in the New Testament, and a promise-fulfillment perspective, in which items in Hebrew Scripture signify certain promises made both to ancient Israelites and to later Christians.[2] Jakobson's linguistic distinctions help us see how Christian revisionary reading shares certain literary features with non-Christian, structuralist accounts of language. Christian revision will be misunderstood, however, if those linguistic features are taken to be sufficient for describing it because structuralist linguistics does not do justice to the category of performance. Although Preus's two perspectives overlap with some features of Jakobson's account, Preus helps underscore the centrality of promise in Christian revisionary reading. Preus's tendency to pit the promise-fulfillment perspective against the shadow-reality perspective is overdone, however; much traditional

Christian revisionary reading of Hebrew Scripture integrates both models into a single, complex strategy of interpretation.

The second part of the chapter examines Paul de Man's understanding of deconstruction in light of the Jakobson and Preus models. I first outline de Man's description of Friedrich Nietzsche's view of the self-deconstructing character of language—its oscillation between assertions it cannot justify and acts it cannot perform. I then compare de Man's description of the self-deconstructing nature of language to Augustine's account of the sign character of Scripture. De Man's claim that language necessarily self-deconstructs turns on his unwarranted assumption that language cannot constitute a fundamentally non-epistemological act. In other words, language oscillates in an undecidable fashion for de Man only because he never really grants to language a performative possibility uncontaminated by epistemology. In contrast, Augustine's account of scriptural signs, while recognizing epistemological dilemmas similar to those de Man observes, makes a place for the actual performance, or use, of language. The category of performance marks a fundamental distinction between de Man's and Augustine's accounts of language: the possibility of a performance that is not epistemological reflects the basic Christian insistence that faith, while it properly seeks knowledge, is not itself an act of knowing.

In the final part of the chapter, after offering a brief overview of Harold Bloom's poetic theory, I compare Bloom's misreading to de Man's deconstruction. Bloom emerges from the comparison as a defender of the irreducible subject's spirit or uniquely creative experience over against poststructuralist efforts to construe such experience as a mode of textuality. I then turn to an assessment of Bloom's effort to bring his theory into relation with some examples of Christian revisionary reading. Possibly in order to evade his own anxiety about the normative claims of rabbinic Judaism, Bloom (as self-professed Jewish gnostic) attacks Christian revision by reducing it to a de Manian conception of pure textuality, a reduction that he otherwise resists when advancing his own theory of poetic revision against de Manian deconstruction. As a result, Bloom attacks an especially weak form of Christian revision in order to evade a stronger form: the Pauline doctrine of justification and the revisionary reading of Hebrew Scripture that it entails. My discussion ends with an irony: Although Bloom tries to evade Pauline theology and revisionary reading, the internal logic of Bloom's own theoretical proposal, especially its insistence on the revisionary experience of the subject, is far more compatible with a Pauline scriptural hermeneutic than Bloom is willing to recognize. Unlike de Man's deconstruction, Bloom's misreading bears to Christian revision what many theologians, both Jewish and Christian, will recognize as an uncanny family resemblance.

The Language of Revisionary Reading

Bridges for dialogue between literary theory and Christian theology are all the more compelling when they can, at least in part, be independently constructed. So it is especially intriguing to find that a structural linguist exploring the linguistic consequences of aphasia and a historian of biblical interpretation examining how Christians have interpreted the Old Testament from Augustine to Luther have arrived at basic models of language and revision with some strikingly analogous features. In his influential essay "Two Aspects of Language and Two Types of Aphasic Disturbances," Roman Jakobson argued that there are two basic ways in which language deteriorates in aphasia, and that these two kinds of disorder point to two fundamental functions of human language. Jakobson observed that aphasia consists of two different sorts of problems: a "similarity disorder" and a "contiguity disorder." A patient suffering from the similarity disorder is able to combine signs but unable to select them. Such a patient can carry on a conversation already in progress by adding items to those selected by the interlocutor, but is unable to begin a dialogue. The opposite situation obtains in the contiguity disorder. Here the patient is unable to construct the syntax of utterances and is reduced to uttering single words or phrases in agrammatical "word-heaps."

Jakobson contended that these two forms of language deterioration reflect two different basic functions of language. Language users select items from among "substitution sets" (groups of signs associated by varying degrees of similarity), and they then combine the selected items so that they become contiguous to one another. For example, in uttering the sentence, "My car is no longer running properly," I select *car* from a substitution set that includes *automobile, vehicle,* and *conveyance,* and I select *running* from a set that includes *not running, operating, functioning,* and perhaps *jogging.* I then combine my selections into a group in which the signs *car* and *running* are contiguously related to each other.

Jakobson went on to associate the two aspects of language (selection and combination) revealed in the two types of aphasia (similarity disorder and contiguity disorder) with two rhetorical tropes, metaphor and metonymy. Metaphor involves selecting one item to stand for another item, while metonymy involves taking an aspect closely associated (contiguous with) an item for the item itself. A patient suffering from the similarity disorder is unable to produce metaphors; one suffering from the contiguity disorder is unable to produce metonymies. Jakobson concluded his essay by arguing that the two aspects of language permeated and helped structure virtually all forms of human culture. He pointed to several large cultural manifestations of the basic metaphor/metonymy contrast: metaphorical constructions predominated in Russian lyrical songs, metonymic constructions in heroic epics; Romanticism and modernism emphasized metaphorical lyric poetry, realism emphasized metonymic narrative prose; surrealism was metaphorical, cubism was metonymic; modern cinematography combined metonymic close-ups and multiple perspectives with metaphoric montage and lap dissolves. Jakobson's conclusion was far-reaching: the metaphor/metonymy distinction appeared to be of "primal significance and consequence for all verbal behavior and for human behavior in general."[3]

In his book *From Shadow to Promise: Old Testament Interpretation from Augustine to the Young Luther*, James Preus outlined what he regarded as two very different Christian approaches to Old Testament interpretation: a shadow-reality perspective and a promise-fulfillment perspective. According to the shadow-reality perspective, Hebrew Scripture consists of representations of material things or historical events that are regarded by Christian interpreters as mere shadows of spiritual realities that are more fully and accurately described in the New Testament. Thus, for example, the Exodus is regarded as a mere shadow of the grace made available in its full reality only in the Christian sacrament of Baptism. Christian readers of Hebrew Scripture adopting this perspective approach their interpretative task entirely from a postincarnational stance. The spiritual things prefigured in Hebrew Scripture are already possessed by Christians by virtue of the incarnation of Christ; consequently, those figures or shadows in Hebrew Scripture no longer have any Christian theological relevance in their own right. Because Baptism now exists, the Exodus has no meaning for these Christian interpreters independent of the baptismal grace it prefigures. As the idiom of spiritual realities and corporeal shadows suggests, this perspective, in many of its historically important forms, was associated with Platonism's distinction between the realms of being and becoming.

Like the shadow-reality perspective, the promise-fulfillment approach to reading Hebrew Scripture also enables Christian interpreters to regard the material realities that Hebrew Scripture describes as references to spiritual realities. This approach construes the relation between material and spiritual realities as a promise, made equally to ancient Israelites and later Christians. Unlike the material realities viewed according to the shadow-reality perspective, these promises are not regarded as mere figures or shadows. As a result, it is no longer the case that Christians have in substance what the Israelites had only in shadowy, less substantial but proleptically Christian form; instead, the same spiritual reality is promised both to ancient Israelites and to later Christians. For example, in one of Martin Luther's formulations, ancient Israelites are promised Christ in his first advent (as Jesus of Nazareth), in his second advent (as the spiritual appropriation of the first advent), and in his third advent (traditionally known as the *parousia* or Christ's second coming). Christians are promised only the second and third advents. Despite the distinction of advents, both Israelites and Christians share a comparable hope. Indeed, from the point of view of the object of the promise, the hope is the same.

The two functions of language observed by Jakobson inform, but do not wholly account for, the two approaches to interpretation described by Preus. The similarity is strongest between the metaphorical function and the shadow-reality perspective: literal meaning is to metaphorical meaning, as shadow is to reality. A more general kind of similarity exists between the way the contiguity or metonymic function favors prose narrative over lyric poetry, and the way the promise-fulfillment perspective requires a continuing plot in which characters receive promises and await their future enactment. But promises and their future fulfillment are performative, and Jakobson's structuralist orientation does not allow him to give sufficient place to the performative character of language. Consequently, Jakobson's categories do not capture the full character of Christian revision.

Jakobson argues that the constituents of any message (what one actually utters) bear an internal relation to language as code, and an external relation to the message itself. Selection involves choosing among items that coexist in language as a timeless code; combination involves the transition from language as a timeless set of possibilities (*langue*) to the realm of language as a speech act (*parole*). In combining, one either joins items in the code to items in the message, or one conjoins items that are in the message. When I say, "My car is not running well," my selection of *car* from the set that includes *automobile* is not a speech act but a mental selection from a timeless set of linguistic possibilities that my language affords me. But when I combine *car* with the other words to form my uttered sentence, I have stepped out of the world of linguistic possibility into the world of actual language use. In the following passage, Jakobson explains why both functions of language—selection and combination—are necessary for communication between persons to be possible:

> The constituents of any message are necessarily linked with the code by an internal relation and with the message by an external relation. Language in its various aspects deals with both modes of relation. Whether messages are exchanged or communication proceeds unilaterally from the addresser to the addressee, there must be some kind of contiguity between the participants of any speech event to assure the transmission of the message. The separation in space, and often in time, between two individuals, the addresser and the addressee, is bridged by an *internal relation:* there must be a certain equivalence between the symbols used by the addresser and those known and interpreted by the addressee. Without such an equivalence the message is fruitless: even when it reaches the receiver it does not affect him.[4]

Here Jakobson makes the provocative claim that the gap between interlocutors is bridged by the atemporal substitution sets that they share. That is, the bridge between persons is constituted by each person's relation to language as *langue*—as timeless set of ever-present linguistic possibilities. Preus's shadow-reality perspective represents a mode of interpretation consistent with selection from such a set of atemporal possibilities. Ancient Israelites either do or do not come to understand that what appears to be a purely temporal reality (say, the Exodus) actually signifies a nontemporal, spiritual good (the grace of Baptism). That is, the addressee (the ancient Israelite) is able or unable to understand the message (Exodus) of the addresser (God) because addressee and addresser share the atemporal substitution set in which Exodus is a metaphor for baptismal grace. Like Jakobson's appeal to the selection pole of language as fundamental to successful communication, the shadow-reality approach to interpretation does not make the passage of time central to understanding. As noted above, a certain sort of Platonic sensibility has historically been associated with the Christian use of the shadow-reality approach. That form of Platonism bears deep affinities with modern structural linguistics: deep structure is to the variable (and inconsequential) surface of language performance, as fixed Platonic forms are to the flux of empirical realities.

It might seem that Jakobson's combination pole, by taking us out of the timeless realm of language as code into the performance of the speech act, is consistent with the promise-fulfillment approach. The promise-fulfillment approach creates contiguity by placing the addressees of the promise in relation to one another because of their common relation to the promiser. Even when written down, promises are made between persons (here, between a personal deity and a believer), not between texts (or between a text and a code). The issue in this case is not whether the Exodus is a metaphor for Baptism, but whether ancient Israelites and later Christians receive the same promise in both Exodus and Baptism. But Jakobson's combination pole differs fundamentally from the promise-fulfillment perspective because it is limited to describing relations between linguistic entities rather than between persons. The promise-fulfillment approach focuses on interpersonal relations of trust, confidence, and hope, rather than on a linguistic relation of shared code or informational message.

If an addresser utters a message to me that is a promise, the significance of that promise *as a promise* cannot be exhausted simply by the fact that I as addressee share a substitution set with the promiser. Confronted with such an utterance, the issue for me is not whether I regard the addresser's "Exodus" as a metaphor for Baptism, but whether I trust the addresser to bring about in the future something that is being promised in the speech act or word-event of the present Exodus. Sharing a code with the promiser is perhaps a necessary but surely not a sufficient condition for regarding the utterance as a promise: I must also put myself in relation to the promiser himself or herself, as one whom I do or do not trust to fulfill those promises. In so placing myself in relation to the promiser, I necessarily step outside Jakobson's structuralist framework (of either code or message) and take up my own personal relation to the person of the promiser. In other words, I cannot do what Jakobson does in the paragraph quoted above: I cannot bridge the gap between persons with an appeal to a shared code (or a message) independent of the addresser.

Jakobson argues that his distinction of metaphor and metonymy marks out ideal poles, and that, in practice, human language and culture actually interrelate the two aspects of language in various complex ways. Nevertheless, he suggests that such linguistic and cultural formations tend to gravitate toward one pole or the other. When read alongside Preus, Jakobson's structuralist understanding of language seems too narrow to capture the range of Christian revisionary reading strategies: he does not attend to the nonstructural, performative dimensions of communication, yet these dimensions prove to be central to Christian interpretation, rooted as it is in a particular interpersonal orientation or stance of faith in a promising deity. This difference between structuralist and Christian assumptions about the kind of experience and language that matters most suggests that post-structuralist accounts of language may prove inadequate for Christian theological purposes.

Reading Preus alongside Jakobson also highlights the overdrawn character of Preus's basic contrast. Preus presents his two perspectives in a polemical, virtually absolutist fashion. He is theologically in favor of Luther's promise-fulfillment perspective and regards the shadow-reality approach as an essentially Platonic hermeneutic that, though embraced by many medieval Christian interpreters, justifiably gave way to the Protestant Luther's emphasis on God's promising Word. But there is no reason why the two models might not be combined, and one can argue (as I will in the next section with reference to Augustine) that, in most instances of Christian interpretation, they have been. To say that two addressees receive the same promise does not mean that the linguistic expression of that situation might not take the form of metaphorical writing that later readers come to interpret in ways less than obvious to earlier readers.

Preus favors the promise-fulfillment perspective in part because of the positive relation it establishes between Judaism and Christianity. The shadow-reality approach regards Old Testament persons according to their similarity to Christ: they are significant only because they are figures or "pictures" of the promised Christ. The promise is itself merely a figure of a reality that others (Christians) possess. As a result, Christian interpreters who follow that model can safely ignore the actual faith of Old Testament persons because Christ is for them the sole model for Christian faith. Now that they have Christ, they have no use for the Old Testament. Such an extreme, Marcionite position would be regarded as heretical by traditional Christian interpreters.

In contrast, the promise-fulfillment approach values the actual expectations and hopes of biblical characters; those characters are not figures of Christ but, like Christians awaiting Christ's second coming, petitioners for him. Such Old Testament persons can become models for Christian faith and hope since they have the same expectation as later Christians. There is, then, a good religious and theological reason for Christians to keep the Old Testament in their Bibles. But in favoring the perspective that stresses Jewish-Christian continuities (and by criticizing the shadow-reality approach that lends itself to Jewish-Christian divergences), the tradition of Old Testament interpretation that Preus celebrates might unduly minimize the revisionary audacity of Christianity. Harold Bloom heaps scorn on Christianity's self-deceiving minimizing of the true agonistic intensity of its own mode of revisionary reading for the sake of Jewish-Christian dialogue. Bloom argues that Christian notions like the fulfillment of one text by another are not only false, but lead Christians to smooth over the deeply antagonistic relation to Judaism that their figurative readings of Hebrew Scripture seem to entail.[5]

To recapitulate: I have suggested that Jakobson's metaphoric pole, in which a selection is made from a vertical substitution set, might easily be viewed as a spectrum of items ranging from reality to shadow. If I come to a text as a revisionary reader taking the shadow-reality approach, I declare that the apparent meaning of a text is only a shadow of its real meaning: this means that I select a term (say, *Baptism*) from that spectrum as a substitution for the prior term (say, *Exodus*). In contrast, Preus's promise-fulfillment perspective on reading takes one out of this bipolar model based on the relation of a single reader to a single text. The promise-fulfillment perspective is not bipolar but triadic, putting several readers of the text into relation with the same promising deity, and therefore into relation with one another. As a result, a Christian revisionary reading, in claiming that the same promise of redemption by Christ is made in the events of Exodus and Baptism, puts Israelites and Christians into a metonymic relation to each other: they are related not because they share something metaphorically (or essentially)—which would make it easy for the Christian reader to set aside the Israelite reader's meaning as redundant—but because both readers stand in relation to the same promising God. Just as they are not essentially related to each other, they are essentially unrelated to the deity since the category of promise presumes no shared essence, but only faith and hope.

Paul de Man's Deconstruction

Paul de Man makes a distinction between tropological and persuasive functions of language. As a system of tropes, language fits both Jakobson's metaphorical function and Preus's shadow-reality perspective. The epistemological relation between de Man's image of the trope and its meaning is essentially the same as that between a metaphor and its meaning, or between an Old Testament shadow and its New Testament reality. In all three cases, the reader is fundamentally a knower, either remaining blind to the true meaning of a text (like ancient Jewish readers of their own Scripture, according to traditional Christian polemic), or overcoming blindness with insight (like ancient Christian readers of Hebrew Scripture, according to their own self-congratulatory ideology). It makes little difference to the similarity between tropes, metaphors, and shadows that where Jakobson and Christian readers discover knowledge, de Manian readers discover only the absence of knowledge.

In "The Rhetoric of Temporality," de Man describes how the language of the most lucid and rigorous Romantic writers deconstructs its own notion of trope as literary symbol; de Man's deconstructive reading allows the very rhetoric of Romantic discourse about the symbol to expose the fraudulence of its own illicit assertion of an intrinsic (metaphorical as opposed to metonymic) relation of image and meaning. In a later essay, "Rhetoric of Persuasion (Nietzsche)," de Man points to a recurring tension in language between its tropological and performative functions. He argues that these two functions work together finally to undermine the performance of language in favor of its (failed) epistemology. But I will argue that what really happens in de Man's argument is that the performative character of language is redefined in epistemological terms, and language as actual performance drops out of his account altogether. By allowing language as possible pure performance to drop out, de Man ends up evading the dynamics of the promise-fulfillment perspective. This evasion reflects de Man's more far-reaching (and ominous) evasion of categories that, by denoting the continuity of personal identity, constitute the basis for promise-making and promise-keeping.[6]

De Man's essay on Nietzsche offers an excellent, though conceptually demanding, introduction to his understanding of the process of deconstruction. Near the essay's end, de Man helpfully summarizes his conclusion, stating it twice:

> . . . the text on the principle of identity [section 516 from *The Will to Power*] established the universality of the linguistic model as speech act, albeit by voiding it of epistemological authority and by demonstrating its inability to perform this very act. But the later text [section 477 from *The*

Will to Power], in its turn, voids even this dubious assurance, for it puts in question not only that language can act rightly, but that it can be said to act at all.

The first passage (section 516) on identity showed that constative language is in fact performative, but the second passage (section 477) asserts that the possibility for language to perform is just as fictional as the possibility for language to assert.[7]

De Man outlines the two-stage movement by which Nietzsche's description enacts, even as it articulates, the deconstructive function of language. Nietzsche first shows that although language may seem to state a knowledge, it actually performs an act; but he then shows that it is just as uncertain that language performs an act. What are the arguments that lead de Man to this circular conclusion?

De Man contends that the pretension of language to offer knowledge of the world is rooted in the principle of noncontradiction: that *A* cannot simultaneously be and not be *A*. This principle underlies the identity principle: that *A* is self-identically *A*. The ability of language accurately to describe the nature of *A* has typically been thought to distinguish philosophical from literary language. Philosophical language—the language of philosophy, mathematics, logic—is able to produce predications (that is, grammatical utterances that link adjectives to subjects) that are accurate descriptions of the way properties relate to the objects that possess them. I make a denominative and constative verbal utterance when, on viewing what appears to me to be a green chair, I say, "This is a green chair." (*Denominative* means that I have given the object a name—I call the object "chair"; *constative* means that this accurately named object is in fact as I have described it—the chair is indeed green.) De Man argues that this philosophical use of language is noncoercive because the actual order of things in the world (that green chair, for example) does not depend on, nor is it affected by, the predicative power of my speech. The self-identical character of that green chair remains the same no matter what I say about it.

But language can work a different way, positing something rather than expressing a knowledge of an object. Here language does not predicate grammatical adjectives of nouns—it actually predicates entities. Language thus performs a genuine act; it does not register an antecedently existing state of affairs, but brings a new state of affairs into existence. An example (not de Man's) may clarify the point. When an umpire shouts "You're out!" he does not describe a state of affairs but brings it into being. Players or coaches who dispute the umpire's call strategically appeal to the contrasting philosophical view of language, insisting that the umpire has misdescribed reality ("You're blind!"). The seasoned umpire will resolutely refuse to take up the challenge on those grounds, instead turning the argument back in the direction of his own reality-producing performance: he has made a judgment call. Although he is an umpire of good judgment and so, consequently, his call is therefore accurate, such accuracy is not the issue. The runner is out because the umpire has declared it so. In the face of excessive protest, the umpire's final recourse is also performative—he throws the protesters out of the game.

De Man, following Nietzsche, is interested in a similar sort of particular, paradoxical positing power of language: the power by which it brings into existence its own appearance as a language that delivers knowledge. De Man's question becomes: How does language act such that it comes to present itself not as acting but simply as describing? De Man argues that language makes this strangely dissimulating move by transforming a metonymy into a metaphor, and thereby turning something contingent into something necessary. The purely contingent, metonymic link between an object and the sensations it gives rise to in its perceiver (for example, the link between the chair and my perception of its greenness) becomes a necessary, metaphoric link between that entity and a concept in the mind of its knower (for example, the link between that green chair and my concept of it as a *green chair*). When I see that green chair, my perception of greenness is, however, only contingently related to the chair: greenness is, at best, a kind of metonymy for the chair. I quickly (and overconfidently) translate my perception into a concept (that of *green chair*), which I falsely take to be a concept that definitively embraces that entity: my utterance "green chair" becomes linked to the object with the strong, necessary bond that de Man associates with metaphors. Nietzsche observes that one could only have assurance of the accuracy (that is, the knowledge status) of that concept if one had first had access to the object apart from the concept. Only if I have some prior way of knowing what the chair is "really" like would I be able to be certain that my concept of *green chair* delivered accurate knowledge of that chair. What I need is a neutral description of the object (in effect, the object's own acccurate self-description) to match against my description. But I cannot say whether I ever had such prior knowledge of that chair: I cannot get outside my concepts any more easily than I can step outside my own skin. Nietzsche's conclusion (according to de Man) is that my conceptual utterances, though they seem to be descriptions affording knowledge, are actually "positional speech acts"—ways in which language performs an act by changing its status as the record of a metonymic sensation into a false status as the apt expression of a metaphoric concept. By such acts, language appears to provide knowledge.

At this point, the argument seems to suggest that, despite appearances to the contrary, language is unavoidably performative. Is the moral of the story, then, simply to set aside our naive confidence in knowledge and accept the inevitability of performance? De Man answers "no," and his answer is crucial for grasping his notion of the deconstructive character of language. He writes: "The text deconstructs the authority of the principle of contradiction by showing that this principle is an act"—this is the point de Man's essay has reached; "but," he continues—and now his essay takes a new turn—"when it [the text] acts out this act, it fails to perform the deed to which the text owed its status as act."[8] In other words, though knowledge first gives way to act, the act itself is not performed.

De Man supports this claim by attending to the precise wording of a passage that he quotes from Nietzsche: "Supposing [*gesetzt*] there were no self-identical A, such as is presupposed [*vorausgesetzt*] by every proposition of logic (and of mathematics), and the A were already mere *appearance*, then logic would have a merely *apparent* world as its precondition [*Voraussetzung*]."[9] De Man has already claimed that the idea that philosophical language is descriptive of the world as it really is results from a prior assumption (*Voraussetzung*). But what one might think would follow from this—that one ought to drop the entire principle of contradiction—is itself put by Nietzsche in the preceding passage in the hypothetical (and therefore positional) mode: "*Supposing* there were no self-identical A" (de Man's emphasis). But, de Man insists, language in the mode of supposition cannot simply trump its epistemological claims. Or, as de Man puts it: "all 'setzen' has been discredited as unable to control the epistemological rigor of its own rhetoric, and this discredit now extends to the denial of the principle of identity as well." De Man here claims to spot what he regards as the telltale sign of "all deconstructive discourse"—it always "states the fallacy of reference in a necessarily referential mode." This necessity is a function of language itself, not of any language user (as though one could control what language does): "deconstruction is not something we can decide to do or not to do at will. It is coextensive with any use of language, and this use is compulsive or, as Nietzsche formulates it, imperative."[10]

The matter can be put a bit differently. Although deconstructive discourse has a negative thrust—saying that language is not a knowledge—the fact that it denies language the status of knowledge does not mean that it affirms that language is an act. The possible positive claim—that language is an act—is undermined by Nietzsche's *gesetzt*, as is the claim that if language is not an act, it must therefore be a knowledge. The failure of language to reach the positive status of act does not impair its negative failure at being a knowledge. Language neither does nor knows, but instead continually presents us with the gap marked out on either side by failed knowledge and failed action. Appealing to Nietzsche's "Course on Rhetoric" near the end of the essay, de Man redescribes this gap as one between rhetoric as a system of tropes and rhetoric as the skills of persuasion (oratory, eloquence). Rhetoric in de Man's view turns out to be neither trope nor performance alone but rather what might be called rhetoricity—an oscillation between language's claim to knowledge (a claim that provides no knowledge because it is actually a performance), and language's seeming performance (a performance that fails to perform but nevertheless makes a claim to knowledge). De Man calls this gap or oscillation between language as constative and language as performative an *aporia*. The *aporia* presents a kind of double paralysis—one seemingly asserts but only acts, one seemingly acts but only asserts—with the result that one never really asserts or acts, but remains continually condemned by language's inherent rhetoricity to try to do both.

I now set aside de Man's view of deconstuction for a moment in order to examine another, ancient view of language: Augustine's *On Christian Doctrine*. This treatise might have been entitled "On Interpreting Scriptural Signs," for in it, Augustine offers a detailed exposition of the sign character of language as used in Scripture and explains to Christians how they should interpret those signs. At first glance, Augustine seems to adopt the shadow-reality perspective in his criticism of the literalism of ancient Israelite interpretation of Scripture. He argues that the root error of such literalism lies in taking a figurative expression (for example, concerning sacrifice) as a sign, but failing to refer the thing signified (for example, "the victims of the flocks and fruits of the earth") to anything else (presumably, Christ's sacrifice). Ancient Israelites thus take the sign for the thing, "so that one is not able to raise the eye of the mind above things that are corporal and created to drink in eternal light."[11] But because the Israelites, unlike the pagans, are adhering to a "usefully instituted sign," they are serving the one true God even when practicing "carnal" rites: "although they took signs of spiritual things for the things themselves, not knowing what they referred to, yet they acted as a matter of course that through this servitude they were pleasing the One God of All whom they did not see."[12]

In this example, Israelite obedience to the literal signs is theologically and religiously efficacious despite an epistemological failure. While this failure leads some to reject Christ's overturning of signs in favor of what they signified, the obedience of others enables them to gain sufficient spiritual training to make the change and be converted. Although Augustine does not emphasize in this passage the promises of the Old Testament, he still transforms the shadow-reality perspective in order to accommodate a sense of the continuity between those Old Testament material signs that were "useful" and the conversion of New Testament persons to the things signified by stressing the spiritual benefit that obedience to those signs affords, even without proper understanding: "On this account Christian liberty freed those it found under useful signs, discovering them to be among those who were 'nigh,' interpreting the signs to which they were subject, and elevating them to the things which the signs represented. From them were constituted the Churches of the holy Israelites."[13] Although they were in "servitude" to the material signs, the patriarchs and prophets were also "spiritual and free" because they did not venerate what they saw but that to which they were referred. They seem similar to later Christians, for whom the useful Old Testament signs have been replaced with the two New Testament signs (sacraments) of Baptism and Eucharist. With proper instruction, the Christian participant in a "useful" sign of the New Testament, much like the patriarchs and prophets, "knows what it refers to so that he venerates it not in carnal servitude but in spiritual freedom."[14]

How much similarity can there be between Old Testament prophets or patriarchs and later Christians? The contrast between spiritual freedom and spiritual servitude seems absolute. In order to be spiritual and free, the patriarchs and prophets must themselves know the real referents of the signs and venerate those spiritual things. But if they know and do this, they become identical to those of New Testament times, thus severing their identity with pre-advent Israel. Such Old Testament spiritual patriarchs and prophets lived "during that time of servitude" in which other, "carnal minds," whose wills were opposed to God, had not yet been the beneficiaries of a revelation of those true referents because they were being "tamed" by the signs themselves.[15] But while the spiritual patriarchs and prophets of the Old Testament were not "carnal," they also were not identical to New Testament Christians; otherwise, there would be no need for their conversion. These Old Testament spiritual persons thus occupy a position between the Old Testament carnal minds and the New Testament spiritual minds. The Old Testament carnal mind does not know that the material sign is a sign; that mind takes it as the material thing it is and nothing more. The New Testament spiritual mind refers the material sign to the spiritual thing it signifies, whether that sign is an Old Testament sacrifice or a New Testament sacrament. Between the two is located the Old Testament spiritual mind, which knows that the material sign is indeed a sign (and hence should not be venerated with respect to its materiality) but does not refer the sign to its proper referent. This Old Testament spiritual mind is an advance over the carnal mind, for "he who does not know what a sign means, but does know that it is a sign, is not in servitude."[16] That is, spiritual freedom exists in embryonic form at the first recognition that certain things are indeed signs.

Although drawing on a sign-thing contrast that at first seems to be simply a version of the shadow-reality perspective, Augustine's account decisively alters that approach by adding the intermediate category of "free and spiritual" Israelites. This category gives the Augustinian scheme an unfolding, progressive character since the three groups read the same signs with increasing insight. Any sort of stark, Marcionite opposition between Old and New Testaments has been broken down; indeed, the discussion is not framed in terms of two texts at all, but rather in terms of a progressive awareness of the single but complexly modulated signifying speech of God (the "Israelites" progress in this awareness, the "Jews" remain unaware).[17] Although Augustine does not characterize that speech as promise in this passage, the continuity that the category of promise provides is established here by the fact that both Israelites and Christians perform the same acts of interpretation of divinely given signs.

The mixed character of Augustine's perspective resembles in some respects de Man's double view of rhetoric as both constative and persuasive. The signs of Scripture are claims to know something (the things signified); in de Man's language, such signs form a constative language, a rhetoric of epistemological tropes. But for Augustine, scriptural signs are also persuasive—they are the means by which God seeks to reorient the attention or wills of the interpreters. Augustine's first class of interpreters (those who fail to recognize the sign character of certain things) are like those whom de Man criticizes for having a naive confidence in their ability to know things. They have made an unwarranted substitution of thing for sign instead of recognizing a purely metonymic link between sign and a thing, a link that is other than the "thingness" of the sign itself. They operate with what de Man calls "misinterpreted systems of relationships."[18] But the third class, the Christian interpreters of the signs, are in the same general epistemological situation. The only difference is that the first group does not know something that the third group knows. Both the absence and presence of knowing are rooted in the same "naive" confidence in the ability of a sign to signify. De Man insists that there can be no continuity or development from the situation of not knowing to that of knowing: "the reversal from denial to assertion implicit in deconstructive discourse never reaches the symmetrical counterpart of what it denies."[19] Instead of the continuity of a reversal that reaches to its counterpart, there is only an interminable oscillation back and forth between knowing and not knowing, between the presence and absence of meaning.

This oscillation occupies the place that Augustine fills with the intermediate category of "free and spiritual" Israelites. But de Man's oscillation represents a situation quite different from the one in which Augustine's spiritual Israelites find themselves. They know that things are signs but do not know what they signify; they have one kind of knowledge and lack another kind. In contrast, de Man's oscillation describes a situation in which "we cannot say that we know . . . [the thing] nor can it be said that we do not know it. What can be said is that we do not know whether or not we know it."[20]

De Man here assumes a first-person point of view on the status of one's knowing. Augustine's account is third person: the spiritual Israelites know one thing and not another. Augustine does not give us a first-person account of how this situation is perceived by the Israelites. Their disposition is likely to be one of expectation or even hope, as they muse to themselves: "I know that this thing is actually a sign signifying something else; I do not know what that something else is, but I am eager to find out." That is, their disposition need not be one of a de Manian undecidability that might beset a hypothetical figure who embodies the perspective of the first group (of carnal Jews) and the third (of Christians). On the contrary, the disposition of expectation is created by the clear sense of what is known (x is a sign of something else) and an equally clear sense that something else is not yet known (that of which x is a sign), together helping define the stance of a particular person.

This line of thought is reinforced by the way Augustine places his discussion of the classes of Jewish readers under the category of servitude rather than under the even less desirable category of error. Error is a decidedly epistemological category, which Augustine reserves for pagan reading. The pagan signs are false, and what they signify is falsely described as divine. But Jewish signs are "usefully instituted" by God; they are a divine rhetoric of persuasion, and Jewish enactment of those signs, with or without knowledge of the things they signify, is a form of servitude or obedience to that divine rhetoric of persuasion. Conversely, Jewish hermeneutical failure reflects a lack of obedience to the divine signifying will (which Augustine, following the Bible, describes as a perverse stubbornness or "hardness of heart"). Augustine's main point is that the reading of signs is inseparably connected with the state of the will—both with the will of God by which the signs have been instituted, and the wills of the readers, who, in responding to the divine will, are enabled to read the signs rightly. Both carnal Jews and spiritual Israelites, at a certain level, have a proper will, even if that will is accompanied by an absent or incomplete knowledge. We might say then that Augustine's signs as a rhetoric of persuasion are effective in establishing continuity, despite the character of that rhetoric as a set of tropes of knowing and not knowing.

We have seen that such an idea of continuity is foreign to de Man's notion of *aporia,* for *aporia* marks the site of an indeterminate oscillation between knowledge and performance. The Augustinian sign does not participate in this *aporia,* precisely because it is a sign and not simply a trope. That is, the sign is a figure of willing or intention on the part of God before it can be understood as a literary trope or meaningful practice. Likewise, a human will lies behind the interpretation of the sign. For Augustine, the process of interpretation is first of all about the relationship of these wills to one another before it is about either the referential character of the sign as a trope or the notion of willing or performance as an "act of the text." De Man's formulation departs from Augustine's at the point where it attributes to act no less than to assertion a referential character. Only by attributing referentiality to both performance and assertion can de Man claim that one always undermines the other: "Performative language is not less ambivalent in its referential function than the language of constatation."[21] De Man's conclusion—that "constative language is in fact performative" but that "the possibility for language to perform is just as fictional as the possibility for language to assert"[22]—would strike Augustine as strange since Augustine introduces "performers" who are independent of the texts that have a capacity to move them because the texts are themselves extensions of a will to signify.

Augustine's reader is able to make the progressive transition or move-ment that de Man says Nietzsche's text cannot make. If de Man's *aporia* both "generates and paralyzes rhetoric and thus gives it the appearance of a history,"[23] Augustine's account of spiritual Israelites offers not the appear-ance of a history but an actual history—of Israelites resisting or accepting a revelation.[24] Augustine's formulation suggests that a change in the opacity of tropes (the new revelation) achieves not a deconstruction but an advance-ment of persuasion: it means that one comes nearer to spiritual things, and proximity allows for divine influence ("thus they were so susceptible to the Holy Spirit"). That is, their wills were susceptible to being moved or per-suaded. Augustine allows, then, for de Man's "two incompatible, mutually self-destructive points of view," but they are not best described as points of view but rather as orientations of will, and they are held by different per-sons or by the same person at different times, not by a single person at the same time (some "stubbornly adhered to such signs as things" since they "could hardly bear it when the time for them to be revealed had come and the Lord condemned them," but others "were susceptible to the Holy Spirit"). The stubborn group does not convert, not because of the insur-mountable obstacle of a text but precisely because the group does not want the obstacle of the text (or tradition) to be surmounted (they reject Jesus because he "did not treat the signs in accordance with the Jewish obser-vance"). These Jews are not in the position of considering the rhetoric of signs as a system of tropes that both give and fail to give knowledge; rather, a given knowledge is rejected, and this rejection, like the acceptance by others, produces not a simulated history, but an altogether real history.

De Man's formulation of the contrast between constative and performa-tive rhetoric differs from Augustine's perspective because de Man never grants to performance a sufficiently independent character to make its sub-version by tropes persuasive. Although it may be the case that "performa-tive language is not less ambivalent in its referential function than the language of constatation,"[25] such a formulation begs the essential question: Is performative language referential precisely as performative? Or does performance instead introduce a category altogether different from epistemology—that is, the category of the enacted will? To say that one's will to establish a referential mode of discourse is undermined by the fact that one's will, rather than knowledge, is what establishes it—and then to say further that this priority of will and lack of knowing does not rule out the claim to know—does not really decide anything about the initiating act itself, *before* that act generates a referential claim. This act as such is not ambivalent—it simply occurs.

In the following passage in which he quotes Nietzsche, de Man works to eliminate this act altogether by means of a moral critique:

"'Thinking,' as epistemologists conceive of it . . . simply does not occur: it is a quite arbitrary fiction, arrived at by singling out one element from the process and eliminating all the rest, an artificial arrangement for the purpose of intelligibility" [Nietzsche]. Whereas the subject results from an unwarranted reversal of cause and effect, the illusion of thought as action is the result of an equally illegitimate totalization from part to whole.[26]

The prose (both Nietzsche's and de Man's) bristles with negative evaluations: the non-act in question is arbitrary, fictional, artificial, unwarranted, illusory, and illegitimate. But the verbs themselves—though cast in passive voice ("arrived at") or gerunds ("singling out," "eliminating"), or turned into nouns ("arrangement," "reversal," "result," "totalization")—do not simply disappear. While thinking may not occur as epistemologists conceive it, some sort of activity is taking place, if only as an act of imagination (according to Nietzsche, "we *first* imagine an act that does not exist").[27] While the referents of such imagination may be fictions, the act of imagination is still an act.

Harold Bloom's Misreading

The act of imagination that de Man regards as a linguistically generated fiction is the very bedrock of Harold Bloom's theory of poetic creativity: that act is "the illusory but always persuasive assertion by the mind of its own powers over all that is not mind, including language."[28] With the word *illusory,* Bloom grudgingly concedes the force of de Man's deconstruction—but with the phrase "always persuasive assertion," Bloom limits its force and assumes his own anti–de Man stance. If de Man's theory is finally about the hegemony of language, Bloom's is about the efforts of those language users called poets to give persuasive expression to their unique imaginative experiences. In direct opposition to de Man, Bloom insists that a trope is always a matter of psychology as well as of language; tropes are the literary manifestations of psychological defenses, and defenses are the psychological way of characterizing the function of literary tropes. To understand this double character of Bloom's tropes, a brief overview of his basic theory of poetic revision is in order. Providing such an overview is not easy; Bloom maps and remaps the process of revisionary reading with arcane terminologies borrowed from all sorts of esoteric discourses: ancient rhetoric, Freudian psychoanalysis, and Jewish mysticism, to name only the three most dominant. Just when one thinks one can follow the map, another book appears, introducing new technical terms or redeploying old ones.

There are several reasons for the baroque complexity of Bloom's critical and theoretical prose style. First, Bloom's theory breaks down any absolute distinction between poetry and critical commentary on poetry: the practical critic of poetry shares the same anxieties of influence that afflict poets, as well as the same wealth of language and imagery. As a result, Bloom's theoretical prose aspires to the dense allusiveness of the poetry it analyzes.

Second, Bloom's critical intelligence functions much like an enormous computer database. Bloom may well have read more (and remembered more of what he has read) than any other living critic and theorist of British and American literature. He seemingly cannot read or use language without instantly invoking a forbidding array of literary and conceptual associations. In many instances, these associations are highly original and idiosyncratic, and Bloom seldom points them out for readers. In effect, he writes for ideal readers who have read as widely and as deeply as he has. Less-than-ideal readers (a group in which I ruefully include myself) can easily miss many of the subtle nuances of his writing.

Finally, those familiar with the writings of Kabbala will not be surprised by Bloom's exploitation of arcane terminological schemes and patterns. Not only does Bloom derive them in large part from his reading of those esoteric Jewish writings, but his own theoretical writings aim to assume a sweeping revisionary stance toward his theoretical precursors, much the way Kabbala sought to revise more traditional interpretations of the Hebrew Bible. In sum, a great deal of the eclectic, shifting, elusive character of Bloom's theoretical prose is not accidental, obscurantist, or the result of a perverse desire to drive his readers to frustration. On the contrary, that is the character of the self-conscious (perhaps too self-conscious), revisionary prose by which Bloom seeks to express a strong, original, and (ideally) unrevisable theory of poetry that is finally much more than a vision of poetry alone.

Although an initial orientation to Bloom's theory requires more than the repetition of slogans ("anxiety of influence," "strong misreading"), we need something much less than a complete discussion of all permutations of the system.[29] Bloom's theory tries to map out the way the patterns of imagery

in any strong poem express the psychological defenses of the poet against
the influences of a precursor's poem. Such "defensive images" are what an
earlier critical generation called poetic allusions—those signs of a poet's
indebtedness to a literary tradition. Bloom insists that these images must
also be understood as rhetorical tropes and psychological defenses. For
example, when a reader encounters imagery of inside and outside in the
poem, he or she is often also confronting the trope of metaphor and, at the
same time and in the same place, so to speak, uncovering a moment of
psychological sublimation on the part of the poet. For an illustration of this
sort of analysis, I turn to Bloom's reading of the opening lines of Wallace
Stevens's early poem "Domination of Black."

> At night, by the fire,
> The colors of the bushes
> And of the fallen leaves,
> Repeating themselves,
> Turned in the room,
> Like the leaves themselves
> Turning in the wind.
> Yes: but the color of the heavy hemlocks
> Came striding.
> And I remembered the cry of the peacocks.
>
> The colors of their tails
> Were like the leaves themselves
> Turning in the wind,
> In the twilight wind.[30]

Bloom analyzes the entire poem (of which I have quoted only the opening lines) in some detail. He works through the six moments that comprise
the unfolding process by which Stevens crafts the poem—a crafting that, in
its allusions to earlier poems (especially to Percy Bysshe Shelley's "Ode to
the West Wind"), subtly tries to revise them. Bloom's discussion of the
opening movement in Stevens's poem (from "clinamen" to "tessera") provides some sense of how his theoretical terminology engages the details of
the poem. *Clinamen* is Bloom's term for the ephebe's *swerve*—the opening
departure from a precursor, the move the poet makes to get his or her new
and original poem off the ground. Shelley's trope of "leaves" is the image
from which Stevens swerves. Here is the opening section of Shelley's poem:

> O wild West Wind, thou breath of Autumn's being,
> Thou, from whose unseen presence the leaves dead
> Are driven, like ghosts from an enchanter fleeing,
>
> Yellow, and black, and pale, and hectic red,
> Pestilence-stricken multitudes: O thou,
> Who chariotest to their dark wintry bed

The winged seeds, where they lie cold and low,
Each like a corpse within its grave, until
Thine azure sister of the Spring shall blow

Her clarion o'er the dreaming earth, and fill
(Driving sweet buds like flocks to feed in air)
With living hues and odours plain and hill:

Wild Spirit, which art moving everywhere;
Destroyer and preserver; hear, oh, hear![31]

Stevens's swerve takes place when the "colors of the bushes / And of the fallen leaves" are found to be "repeating themselves." This is an image of presence and absence: the leaves are present as shadows cast by firelight, yet precisely as shadows they literally fail to repeat themselves and hence are absent as colors. Stevens's alteration of Shelley's trope becomes a trope of irony, meaning the opposite of what it says: the poem says that the colors repeat themselves, and yet means that they do not really repeat themselves (in contrast to Shelley's "yellow, and black, and pale, and hectic red"). This moment is also a moment of psychic defense on the part of Stevens, who is manifesting a reaction formation, a defense against a repressed desire (in this case, death, imagined as the absence of color) that takes the form of "a reaction against that desire" (in this case, the perpetuation of life, imagined as the presence of color). In this way, Bloom charts the first, "emptying out" or "limiting" movement of Stevens's poem, which then receives its answering, provisionally completing movement, called "tessera." The poetic image here is "the heavy hemlocks," which function as parts for a whole (that is, as a synecdoche) that is death itself. Psychically, the poet has here turned against the result of the reaction formation (life) with an image of death. The poem then moves into its second working out of the triadic pattern, as this achieved image of death is itself undone (as part-for-whole synecdoche gives way to the less intrinsic associations of metonymy), and as the dark figure of the hemlocks gives way momentarily to the turnings in the room of the colors of the peacocks. Bloom then proceeds to chart the remaining moments in the poem's revisionary reading of its poetic precursors.

As early as his review of Bloom's first explicit presentation of his theory in *The Anxiety of Influence*, Paul de Man rejected Bloom's view of tropes as psychological events, insisting that tropes always can be reduced (or, in fact, always reduce themselves) to purely linguistic entities.[32] Bloom observes that the de Manian *aporia* that a text reveals on a deconstructive reading marks a moment at which persuasion "yields to a dance or interplay of tropes." Bloom argues that this deconstructive moment is unwarrantably reductive—a futile attempt "to see poetry as being a conceptual rhetoric, and nothing more." Bloom even hints at de Man's underlying strategic (if not opportunistic) rationale for such reductiveness: "Rhetoric, considered as a system of tropes, yields much more readily to analysis than does rhetoric considered as persuasion, for persuasion, in poetry, takes us into a realm that also includes the lie."[33]

Bloom's first move against de Man is always to go him one better: when de Man announces that he has found a failed epistemological moment, Bloom declares that de Man has simply produced a new trope. Bloom argues that de Man cannot really escape the character of trope in favor of epistemology, for "all is trope save in games." If all is trope, then every concept of trope is itself a trope, and that applies even to those concepts of trope that declare tropes to be solely epistemological instruments. De Man's key move, argues Bloom, is to redefine "poetic thinking *as* the process of rhetorical *substitution* rather than as a thinking by [a] particular trope."[34] This redefinition requires de Man to separate the psychological genesis of a trope from the resulting process that is triggered: the resulting process is presented as one of substitution, but Bloom insists that even the prior psychological act is tropic. Bloom argues that de Man's ascetic view of trope illegitimately ("too purifyingly") separates the trope from the *topos* ("place" or "commonplace") that generated it.[35]

Bloom's appeal to the origin or *topos* of the trope is not equivalent to a philosophical appeal to foundations. On the contrary, Bloom charges de Man with a naive foundationalism: Bloom argues that it is de Man who believes that tropes exist. But, remarks Bloom, like every critic, de Man "necessarily tropes the concept of trope, *for there are no tropes*, but only concepts of tropes or figures of figures."[36] To say, as de Man implies, that tropes exist is, from Bloom's perspective, to misspeak: tropes cannot be said to exist (literally, to "stand out") unless one has already made a trope/ nontrope (or nonliteral/literal, foreground/background) distinction. This is precisely the distinction that Bloom denies. For Bloom, it is tropes "all the way down," since at the root is not something literal that the trope turns away from into nonliterality; rather, at the root is only a successful or unsuccessful act of will. "Trope" is the way we name that act of will insofar as it becomes figured in language. Language itself, then, is simply a collection of figurations of will.[37] Unlike the tropes it generates, the will is irreducible. For Bloom, a trope is always one of two things: a will that translates itself into verbal act (and thus figures one's character, or *ēthos*), or a will that fails to make this translation (and thus figures one's desire, or *pathos*). His point is that, in either case, "a trope is a figure of will rather than a figure of knowledge."[38]

Where does the trope's will reside? To pursue that question is to begin to measure the price Bloom has paid for his self-described humanistic resistance to de Man's reductionist textuality. Against de Man, Bloom insists that the will that produces a trope lies behind, or prior to, language; the trope is "a cut or gap made in or into the anteriority of language." What is anterior to language? Time, for language is itself only a "figurative substitution for time." So the will first enacts itself in time, producing a trope that cuts into language. And where does time reside? Time resides nowhere—time is simply this fallen cosmos in which the poet finds himself suffocating, and in the midst of which he wills to utter in defiance of time—to "lie against time." Bloom calls this will to utter or lie against time "misprision" or "misreading" since it necessarily takes the form of reacting against a preexisting will or lie. Indeed, the process of misreading is what constitutes any text. Bloom regards texts not so much as linguistic structures as instances of *"the will to utter within a tradition of uttering."* "Misprision is the process by which the meanings of intentionality trope down to the mere significances of language, or conversely the process by which the significations of language can be transformed or troped upward into the meaningful world of our Will-to-Power over time and its henchman, language."[39] Misprision is fundamentally a stance, and stance cannot be reduced by de Man to language itself because a stance is first assumed prior to language in an act of will seeking to gain the upper hand over time.

Pursuing the regression—from language, to time, to a will-to-power over time—reveals the price Bloom has paid in order to secure a nondeconstructible stance. I have called that price hyperspirituality—a deeply anti-incarnational stance. Bloom insists on the irreducibility of subjectivity or the human spirit to the prison-house of language: "The imagination . . . has no referential aspect. It has no meaning in itself because it is not a sign; that is, there is no other sign to which it can relate or be related. Like the *En Sof* or Infinite Godhood of Kabbalah, the imagination stands above and beyond the texts that would invoke it."[40] But in standing above texts, the human imagination also stands above all else: history, culture, the body. The imagination is freed from reduction to textuality only by becoming a radically disincarnate spirit, a spirit whose task it is to liberate itself from all forms of constraining necessity. Such a spirit can only regard incarnation as it does creation itself—as a terrible fall away from the realm of the divine fullness or *plērōma* into the suffocating morass of the materialistic *kenōma* or emptiness of the world as we know it: "The poet is our chosen man, and his consciousness of election comes as a curse; again, not 'I am a fallen man,' but 'I am Man, and I am falling'—or rather, 'I *was* God, I *was* Man (for to a poet they were the same), and I *am* falling, from myself.' "[41] In order to recover from his fall-as-incarnation, the ephebe must disincarnate himself by rendering his poetic precursor incarnate. In the revisionary strategy that Bloom (inverting Saint Paul) cunningly calls *kenōsis*, the ephebe reads (tropes upon) the precursor in order to force him to "give up his godhead" so it can be claimed by the ephebe for himself. Together with the counter-balancing strategy called *daemonization,* the ephebe's kenotic troping humanizes the precursor while divinizing himself.[42]

Bloom finds the paradigmatic illustration of the incarnation of the precursor by means of the disincarnation of the ephebe at the outset of John Milton's *Paradise Lost.* There Satan becomes Bloom's archetypal strong poet by disavowing the incarnation of God and proclaiming the radically disincarnate character of his own strong spirit:

> The incarnation of the Poetic Character in Satan begins when Milton's story truly begins, with the Incarnation of God's Son and Satan's rejection of *that* incarnation. Modern poetry begins in two declarations of Satan: "We know no time when we were not as now" and "To be weak is miserable, doing or suffering."[43]

Elsewhere, Bloom describes William Blake's "State of Milton"—the Poetic State—as one of self-purgation or self-annihilation, one "in which the Spectre [that which blocks all creativity, that is, the condition of having been created by another] is cast off by the awakened humanity [the spirit] in a man." To enter that state is not to give up godhead for death on a cross, to find one's power made perfect in weakness, or to bear on one's body the marks of Christ—but "to cast off . . . everything that can die, every mortal encrustation."[44] In sum, then, for Bloom poetic spirit lives only by means of tropes of radical disincarnation or hyperspirituality.

In defending the freedom of this spirit against de Man's hypertextuality, Bloom is forced to take "the poet in a poet" out of the embodied realm of history and culture altogether. While insisting against de Man on the utter irreducibility of the poetic spirit, Bloom (in a move that illustrates his self-conception as a revisionary theorist) reserves a subordinate place within his theory for de Man's efforts to read will as language: "I would agree with Paul de Man that all strong poems contain an authentically self-negating element, a genuinely epistemological moment, but always I would insist that this moment comes in *their relationship to a prior poem,* a relationship that remains inescapably subject-to-subject centered."[45] But the subjects in question have become exceedingly thin—spirits now free because they lack bodies.

When Bloom brings his hyperspiritualist theory of revision to bear on Christian revisionary reading of Scripture, he characterizes Christian revision almost exclusively from the shadow-reality perspective. But we have seen that classical Christian revisionary reading, represented by Augustine, for example, combines the shadow-reality and promise-fulfillment perspectives in order to develop a complex account of the continuity and discontinuity between Judaism and Christianity. In characterizing Christian revision one-sidedly from the shadow-reality perspective, Bloom chooses to disregard the extent to which his model of poetic influence is analogous to Christian interpretative models that invoke some form of the promise-fulfillment perspective. Both the promise-fulfillment perspective and Bloom's view of rhetoric as a means of persuasion are volitional: whether the believer/reader trusts the promise and whether the promise-maker honors that promise do not turn on what either one knows, but on the kind of consistent intention and action pattern, or character, they display.

Yet Bloom takes on a weak precursor in the form of a shadow-reality version of Christian revision, rather than the stronger precursors that take more seriously Christianity's relation to Judaism because he wishes to distance his theory from traditional Judaism. He does so in sublimated fashion by distancing his theory from a traditional Christianity that would be intrinsically related to that Judaism. Bloom avoids Judaism by avoiding the triadic character of the promise-fulfillment perspective. The meaningfulness of the horizontal relation of discontinuity between ancient Israelites and Christians is made possible only by a set of isomorphic vertical relations: A is like B enough to be meaningfully discontinuous with B simply because A, like B, is related to C; Paul is like Moses enough to be importantly unlike him because both Paul and Moses respond to the promises of the same God.

Bloom's criticism of Christian usurpation of Hebrew Scripture as "their" Old Testament is not altogether misplaced, however; the history of Christianity can provide Bloom with easy targets that will let him escape Christianity's relation to Judaism. Some early comments by Luther on Psalm 51 represent the sort of interpretation that Bloom opposes.[46] Luther was later to change his interpretation of the psalms, bringing them under the promise-fulfillment perspective that he was beginning to develop. Consequently, Luther's later interpretation (to which we will turn below) is much less open to Bloom's objections (and closer to Bloom's own concerns).

In his earlier interpretation of the psalm, Luther observes that David, the psalm's speaker, comes to "accuse himself," an accusation that justifies David because it brings him into agreement with the judgment of God, in contrast to Saul, who defends himself when rebuked by Samuel (in 1 Sam. 15:17-21).[47] Luther suggests that the church (in whose "person" David speaks) engages in a self-accusation that serves as a self-justification, while the synagogue (symbolized by the unrepentant Saul) engages in a self-defense that serves as a reason for its condemnation. In Luther's reading, David's prophetic speech takes him out of his immediate historical context into that of the later church, while Saul's speech turns him into a symbol of the later synagogue. Luther formulates the distinction between church and synagogue according to the contrasting responses to divine judgment by the Hebrews David and Saul (represented by their respective responses to the condemnations of Nathan and Samuel). But while Saul's negative response is presented as his own work, David's positive response is presented not as a response of a historical person but of the church. Luther seems to signal this distinction when he contrasts David's speaking "prophetically" with Saul's being a "symbol." As a result, the contrast of spirit versus letter with which the passage ends cannot really be a contrast made within Hebrew Scripture as long as one character (David) can speak his part of the contrast only by stepping prophetically outside that text. Instead, the text of the Hebrew Bible remains a mere letter that is effectively displaced by the spirit of the New Testament church.

To Bloom, this sort of revisionary reading of the Hebrew Bible is only a version of an even more pervasive and loathsome idealizing reading: "In merest fact, and so in history, no text can fulfill another, except through some self-serving caricature of the earlier text by the later. To argue otherwise is to indulge in a dangerous idealization of the relationship between literary texts . . . [and this is to] refuse the temporal anguish of literary history."[48]

When Luther returned to his study of the psalms somewhat later, he reconceived David's role. In his later reading, Luther does not idealize the relation between Hebrew Scripture and the New Testament in the way that Bloom objects to; rather, Luther repositions the letter/spirit distinction within Hebrew Scripture itself. In doing so, Luther makes David's spiritual experience—his self-accusation and repentance at Nathan's word of judgment—one that he could have had as a historical individual in his own time and place. Luther has now come to view Hebrew Scripture not simply as the strong literary precursor of the Christian New Testament, but as a document produced by an authentic religious struggle all its own: in this instance, by the psalmist's own historical and faithful struggle with God. The category of promise that Luther came to emphasize creates a relationship between a precursor of Christianity like David and subsequent Christian readers of the Psalms. This relationship is not the replacement of the first by the second (as in Jakobson's substitution set, de Man's epistemological trope, or Preus's shadow-reality perspective); nor is it based on an interpretative struggle between David and the later Christian believer (or between David as the author of the Psalms and Luther as their interpreter). Instead, it is the consequence of the relation to God that David shares with later Christians because all of them are recipients of the same divine promise.

The convergences and divergences between Bloom's theory and Luther's revisionary readings, like Bloom's hyperspiritualist inversion of incarnation, suggest that Bloom's portrayal of his revisionary ratio of *kenōsis* as a *"dae-*

monic parody" of Christianity may not be off target.[49] The question is whether Bloom's parody, like most parodies, gains much of its independent plausibility only when directed against a one-sided or distorted target. How would things look if one began by rejecting Bloom's governing usurpation—the usurpation of theology by poetry—and started from the opposite assumption: that while ancient poetry may precede theology chronologically, modern poetic theory is, both chronologically and conceptually, largely a surrogate theology? What if Bloom were then to confront his theory's own precursor (Christian revisionary reading) in its strongest form?

Such a confrontation would have the merit of fulfilling one of Bloom's imperatives. Bloom announces that he prefers to read poets such as Ralph Waldo Emerson at their "strongest" rather than at their "most prevalent."[50] He also states that "the interpretation of a poem necessarily is always interpretation of that poem's interpretation of other poems. . . . To interpret a poem, necessarily you interpret its difference from other poems. Such difference, where it vitally creates meaning, is a family difference, by which one poem expiates for another."[51] Scholar of American literature Sacvan Bercovitch argues that Emerson stands solidly within, even as he reinterprets, American Puritanism; Bloom explicitly rejects Bercovitch's interpretation, preferring to see Emerson as a wholehearted opponent of that tradition.[52] There is, I will suggest, a revealing parallel between Bloom's scorn for a Puritan Emerson and his evasion of a Bloomian Paul. Bloom proclaims: "Know each poem by its *clinamen* and you will 'know' that poem in a way that will not purchase knowledge by the loss of the poem's power."[53] Does Bloom really wish to know the Christian poem according to its clinamen—its particular swerve from its Jewish precursor? Or does he purchase a certain knowledge of Christian revision precisely by means of an emptying out of the Christian poem's power, as well as the power of the Judaism from which it swerved?

Bloom begins his essay "Before Moses Was, I Am" by making totalizing pronouncements, pointing to "that Christian act of total usurpation" and concluding that, in the Christian effort to save the Old Testament, "that is precisely what they saved—*their* Old Testament."[54] The key instance of usurpation on which Bloom focuses is the way the statement of Jesus ("Before Abraham was, I am," John 8:58) plays upon God's announcement to Moses in Exod. 3:14: "I AM WHO I AM." Bloom's conception of total Christian usurpation contrasts sharply with his usual procedure of analyzing influence from the ephebe's rather than from the precursor's point of view. In this case, Judaism should be the precursor, Christianity the ephebe, and one would expect Bloom to assess the Christian ephebe's success in overcoming the oppressive weight of its strong precursor. Instead, Bloom begins by announcing what remains of the precursor in the ephebe—and the answer seems to be nothing.

Bloom may make this opening move because if nothing of the precursor Judaism remains in the ephebe Christianity, he need not worry that an attack on Christian revision might reimplicate him with Judaism. Consequently, in the case of Christian revision of Hebrew Scripture, Bloom seems to rule out from the beginning one obvious source of the precursor's pressure for continuity that the ephebe must resist: the religious pressure to continue to obey Jewish law felt by those Jews who believed that Jesus was the promised Messiah. Bloom insists that any pressures toward continuity of this sort are literary and poetic, not religious or theological:

> . . . I am going to read a number of John's namings of Moses as being tropes more for the text than for the supposed substance of what the New Testament (following the Septuagint) insists upon calling the Law. I myself will call it not Torah but J or the Yahwist, because that is where I locate the agon. Not theology, not faith, not truth is the issue, but literary power, the scandalous power of J's text, which by synecdoche stands for the Hebrew Bible as the strongest poem that I have ever read in any language I am able to read.[55]

But Bloom's clinamen or swerve from Torah to text does not so much locate the agon as displace it—or, rather, it recasts the intrareligious struggle between John and the Torah-giver Moses as an intratextual struggle between John and the writer J (the Yahwist). Considering John and Paul from the purely literary point of view of his poetic theory, Bloom admits John to the canon of strong misreaders because John's Jesus deploys the revisionary trope of *transumption* or *metalepsis* (which depicts what is later as what is earlier), but he exposes Paul as a despicably weak reader, one who cannot "lie against time" at all but only "against the text."[56] Yet despite his announced intentions, Bloom's treatment does not remain simply literary, but keeps slipping into religious realms. Such slippage finally allows Bloom to deem John, but not Paul, to be anti-Semitic. Bloom suggests that John's anti-Semitism can be separated from his power as revisionary reader, while Paul's revision of Judaism is essentially linked to textual ineptitude or pure bad faith as a reader. What Bloom apparently cannot tolerate is the possibility that Christian revision of Judaism might be an instance of strong misreading.[57]

A principal source of the struggle between ancient Jewish Christians and ancient non-Christian Jews was the status of what those who followed Paul called *nomos* or law. For them, the post-Christian import of Jewish law was an unavoidable issue if one wished to justify a Christian deviation from other Jewish interpretations of a divinely given Torah. Does Bloom take up this Jewish-Christian controversy because he is fundamentally (however subconsciously) concerned to justify his own Jewish gnostic swerve away from orthodox Judaism? If so, perhaps one can understand why it might be advantageous to replace the question of the law with the issue of priority and authority: one could then swerve from normative Judaism by means of pitting one text against another while avoiding altogether the religious question of the meaning and significance of Torah observance itself.

Something like this may explain why Bloom can find in the Gospel of John a strong "lie against time" that is connected not with John's anti-Semitism but rather with a weak "lie against the text." As Bloom reads it, the transumption or metalepsis of John's Jesus' utterance, "before Abraham was, I am" (John 8:58), is about priority and authority and absolutely not about the law as such. If it were, Bloom might have been more interested in Moses (in reality, a lawgiver, not a writer), the implied object of Jesus' transumption of Abraham. But Bloom interprets Jesus' implied religious transumption of Moses as essentially John's poetic or literary effort to go behind Moses to the writer-poet J. In moving so quickly from Moses to J, Bloom disregards the implied struggle with the status of Jewish law represented by Jesus' trope; Bloom chooses to admire it, he says, for its "literary power" rather than for its "supposed substance." But in the case of Paul's "lie against the text" of Exod. 34:29-35 (by claiming in 2 Cor. 3:12ff. that Moses veils his face in order to hide its fading splendor), the specifically religious issue is so central that Bloom is moved to declare his theory inapplicable to what Paul is doing: unlike John, Paul simply "lies against the text." Now clearly, John's having Jesus say "before Abraham was, I am," as a trope upon the troping speech of God in Exod. 3:14 ("I AM WHO I AM") has a rhetorical subtlety quite different from Paul's insistence that Moses veiled his face because its splendor was fading. Paul's declaration does not trope against the prior trope of veiling but rather gives a religious reason for it, which Bloom thinks goes against—"lies against"—the text.

Bloom's categories simply do not do justice to the full biblical account in Exodus, which Paul regards not as a text but as a religious event of revelation. The biblical story provides a textual opening for an obvious question: If the people are initially afraid to approach Moses because of the brilliance of his glowing face (Exod. 34:30), why are they suddenly (and without explanation) able and willing to do so (Exod. 34:31-32)? Perhaps the people's eyes have adjusted to the light. If so, why does Moses put the veil back on after speaking to them (Exod. 34:33)? As a trained midrashic reader, Paul easily exploits these textual opportunities to offer his own account of the event's religious meaning: Moses wants to hide from his followers evidence that the splendor of his face is fading. But Bloom does not want to engage the provocative Pauline religious claim that an effort to secure righteousness through obedience to Torah leads to spiritual death. Bloom prefers instead to say that Paul, who rarely "gets any text right," here misrepresents Torah and "confounds the law with death" in order to conclude perversely that "the law is death." Bloom's claim that Paul "confounds the

law with death" is especially revealing in light of what Bloom says elsewhere about fulfillment: "For us, now, the only text that can fulfill earlier
texts, rather than correct or negate them, is what ought to be called the text
of death. . . . "[58] But something analogous to this seems to be Paul's own
claim: that to attempt to fulfill the text (of Hebrew Scripture) with another
text (the law) is to succumb to a kind of spiritual death. For Paul, the law is
indeed a text of death, though not by virtue of its inherent character (Bloom
himself seems unable to get Paul's text right when he says that Paul claims
that the law "is" death), but by virtue of what Paul believed to be its
changing role in the divine economy of salvation.

Elsewhere, Bloom argues that the sort of spiritual struggle represented
by this Pauline attitude toward Jewish law lies at the heart of all interpretative struggles that, in opposition to de Man's effort to reduce psychology to
language, remain as much a matter of psychic defenses as of literary tropes.
Bloom admits that the basic movement underlying his six revisionary ratios
and threefold dialectic of revision is historically a "displacement of a Protestant pattern" that goes back to "similar triads of the spirit in the Psalms
and the Prophets, and in Job."[59] This triad—of crisis, felt inadequacy, and
hope of recovery—seems much like the triad evoked by Paul's struggle with
the law, the struggle leading to his "strange" reading of Exodus 34. It is
tempting, but ultimately mistaken, to conclude that Bloom's quarrel is with
orthodox Christianity rather than with orthodox Judaism. The Christian
engagement with Jewish law is precisely the kind of relation that might lend
itself to description as a struggle between meanings generated by the differ-
ing stances or orientations of persons, rather than a struggle between texts
and their meanings. Indeed, in his specific position as Pharisaic Jew obedi-
ent to the Torah who becomes the Christian Jew by means of a reconception of Torah (see Romans 9–11), Paul assumes the stance of one who
"measure[s] his stance in regard to his precursor's stance"—that is, in regard
to his own former self.[60]

Has Bloom's construal of Christian revisionary reading been so reductive
as to partake in some way of that lie that all poems make? This question is
not as impertinent as it first appears; Bloom himself anticipates the possibility—though not, perhaps, with the precise religious application I am
giving it. "Poems," says Bloom, "lie primarily against three adversaries":
themselves, other poems, and time.[61] Given Bloom's insistence that there
are no qualitative differences between poets and critics, it seems that the
same possibility of lying might be true—or even more true—of strong
critics. In his reading of the Christian "poets" John and Paul, does Bloom
"lie against himself" (that is, as heir of the orthodox Jewish tradition)? Is
Bloom, like Milton's Satan, "surprising enough to be a universal prodigal
son"?[62] He continues: "We believe the lies we want to believe because they

help us to survive. Similarly, we read (reread) the poems that keep our discourse with ourselves going. Strong poems strengthen us by teaching us *how to talk to ourselves,* rather than how to talk to others."[63]

> But I read Wordsworth pretty much in the personal way I read the Hebrew Bible, looking for consolation, by which I don't mean cheering myself up. As the years pass, I develop an ever greater horror of solitude, of finding myself having to confront sleepless nights and baffled days in which the self ceases to know how to talk to itself. Wordsworth, more than any other single poet, instructs me in how to sustain the heaviness of going on talking to myself.[64]

Is Bloom's reading of Christian revision a particular kind of lie he tells for his own survival—a lie to keep himself going? Would a genuine conversation with the "other" in this instance weaken his survival—at least in the terms of his present self-understanding as Jewish gnostic?

One wonders whether Bloom has really applied to Christian revision his notion of texts "not as linguistic structures but as instances of *the will to utter within a tradition of uttering.*"[65] Bloom can criticize the work of "conceptual rhetoricians" like de Man because their notion of trope "does not interpret this war between text and intentions but fights instead on the side of text."[66] Bloom seems to makes a similar move, however, when he confronts Christian revision; he also begins to fight on the side of text (the Hebrew Bible) rather than "interpret this war"—and this despite one commentator's claim that Bloom sees "the war for authenticity and finality between surface (text) and depths (intentions variously clear and dark) as a true struggle of contraries."[67] To argue on the side of text alone, declares the gnostic and Kabbalistic Bloom, is to side "with the Talmudists against the Kabbalists." But when the Kabbalists are Christian, Bloom's own reading seems to become oddly talmudic (see his telling appeal to rabbinic authority at the end of "Before Moses Was").[68]

Bloom's poet's anxiety is an anxiety about one's belatedness in relation to the precursor. It is an anxiety about, and effort to resist, the realm of necessity, the tyranny of time's "it was." The ephebe's act of resistance takes the form of a lie against time. The lie is a false but heroic assertion of originality, an assertion that is both trope and psychic defense against belatedness. The trope resists time's tyranny by turning away from the literal meaning of that against which it turns (though this meaning is, of course, not really literal, but is itself a prior trope). Originality thus demands a trope; origins, insists Bloom, are always tropes, and nothing but tropes. The trope is false because it insists that what it turns toward is the literal image's true and exclusive meaning; but the next reading of this trope will prove this claim false by turning once again.

Bloom's complaint against time's "it was" might be compared to Luther's comment on Psalm 102, as one final instance of the deep convergence and divergence between Bloom's and Christian revision. Luther writes:

> . . . the whole psalm is the complaint of a faithful people or of any soul groaning about its old age and the law of sin, looking toward the newness of grace, which is in Christ, for whose coming it prays. Thus Rom. 7:24-25 says: "Wretched man that I am! Who will deliver me from the death of this body?. . . The grace of God through Jesus Christ."[69]

Regarding David's lament in verse 5 ("Because of my loud groaning my bones cling to my skin"), Luther writes:

> So the apostle argues well in Rom. 7:18-20: "To will is present with me," and "what I do not will, this I do, etc." where we have the same complaint as in this psalm.
>
> Every truly contrite person finds himself to be such a person, since he finds himself to be extremely weak toward the good and inclined toward the evil.[70]

The psalmist's anxiety arises when he finds himself "to be extremely weak toward the good and inclined toward the evil." Like the later Paul, the psalmist is anxious and, "'forgetting what lies behind and straining forward to what lies ahead' (Phil. 3:13), looks only to the future and in a state of consternation (Ps. 116:11) sees himself extremely humiliated and every man a liar."[71] Do the anxieties of Bloom's misreader and Luther's psalmist have anything in common? Does Bloom's misreader's "lie against time" have anything to do with the lies of those described by the psalmist?

Although the anxiety of both is bound up with time, the misreader looks to the tyranny of time, the psalmist to the tyranny of his own evil. The psalmist turns from past to future, but the future looks equally bleak because his past evil seems so insurmountable that the future seems as though it will be no different from the past: "For to such people, even if many days are still left to them, they seem already to have passed"[72]—that is, to those who are thrown into consternation and humiliation when they see themselves in the presence of God. Insofar as he does not come to this recognition, the psalmist tells a lie regarding time. He says: I still have many days left to me (in other words, the time of contrition has not run out). But this is a lie because time, insofar as it is the context for repentance, is defined by the divine perspective in which even the future becomes past: "Thus Ps. 90:4 says: 'A thousand years in Thy sight are as yesterday which is past, and as a watch in the night.'" So if Bloom's misreader lies against time by denying time's "it was," Luther's psalmist lies against time by denying that the time that will be is anything other than the time that was. Put another way, the misreader regards time solely as the realm of necessity (what has been done), rather than the realm of freedom (what might be possible). Time for the misreader is to be resisted, while time for the contrite psalmist is to be welcomed as the offer of a new possibility. Such recognition of time's possibilities requires that the psalmist assume a stance not first with respect to time, but to God. In assuming this perspective, the psalmist must regard time as reduced to a single dimension—to atemporality—with respect to God. The psalmist pours out his supplication "before the Lord":

> But no one is "before the Lord" except one who has his back not only to past and present days but also to the future ones. For there he sees them for what they are before God. Before him, however, are all the past and used up days. But he who turns his face to these days and his back to God thinks that they are something.[73]

Luther draws an absolute contrast between a (false) regard of temporality and a (proper) stance "before God." Bloom reports that William Wordsworth's teaching ("how to sustain the heaviness of going on talking to myself") is crucially different from the theistic teaching of Augustine: "*The Prelude,* like its nearest ancestor, *Paradise Lost,* is not an Augustinian poem. Saint Augustine after all shared the universe with God, but Milton and Wordsworth were quite alone in the cosmos."[74] Luther's psalmist, struggling with the righteousness of God, like Paul struggling with the righteousness of Torah, raises a critical question for Bloom: Is the power of poetic revision purely aesthetic—or do its roots lie much deeper, perhaps even in the strong theorist's own resistance-by-sublimation to the stance of the Yahwist, strong precursor, toward God?

2

Text and Performance

Christian theologians typically claim that the Word of Scripture, like the sacrament of the Eucharist, is a means through which the Spirit makes the risen Christ present to believers. Some Romantic writers such as Samuel Taylor Coleridge and Johann Wolfgang von Goethe transformed Christian conceptions of eucharistic presence into secular, literary claims about the intimate relation of meaning to image in poetic symbols. In his early deconstructive reversal of Coleridge's elevation of symbol over allegory, Paul de Man attacks what he regards as the Romantic symbol's illicit assertion of the presence of meaning in an image as a barely disguised secular surrogate for the Christian claim that Christ is present in the Eucharist. There is good reason, then, to turn to debates about the Eucharist as an especially promising context for examining some of the theological implications of de Man's exposure of the self-deconstructing character of the rhetoric of Romanticism. In the first part of this chapter, I consider one example of Christian debate about the sacrament, Martin Luther's treatise on the Lord's Supper. In discussing the Eucharist, Luther seeks, like de Man, to avoid idolatrized conceptions of presence, but unlike de Man, he also resists any move to utter absence. Luther moves between the extremes of idolatrizing presence and atheistic absence by invoking the notion of performance at crucial points in his argument, and by drawing on the ancient christological formulation of the Creed of Chalcedon for rules by which to think and speak with theological propriety about the character of divine presence.

De Man can be explicit about the way deconstructive reading, in its very resistance to idolatry, opposes the Christian concept of incarnation. For example, in an essay on Jean-Jacques Rousseau's novel *Julie ou la Nouvelle Héloïse*, he challenges Julie's notion of a wholly transcendent God who is then made incarnate; he observes that she has "anthropomorphized" God in order to receive from God "the same attributes of selfhood and of will . . . that she requested from Saint-Preux."[1] He chastises Julie for addressing an "overself that does not differ from her in kind," a perspective that for him simply reiterates the idolatrous incarnational ideal represented by the symbol's pretense of continuity between "signs and their signification."[2] Unmasking that pretense, de Man insists that texts do not signify meanings; rather, the rhetoricity of language—the play of signifiers—continually works to ensure the absence of all meaning. The result is a futile epistemological situation in which, although nothing substantive can be known, the reader is constantly seduced into thinking that it can. In the second part of this chapter, I explore this situation by contrasting de Man and Jacques Derrida as readers of Walter Benjamin's essay "The Task of the Translator." A comparison of readings by de Man and Derrida suggests that there are two kinds of absence: one in which x might be present but is not, and one in which x never has been, never will be, and never could be present. These absences look very different from an incarnational perspective. The first absence, proclaimed by Benjamin and Derrida, may lead to a secular but not antireligious *via negativa* (negative path, or way of characterizing the deity by saying what the deity is not). The second absence, announced by de Man in his comments on Benjamin's essay, reflects a radical and nonparadoxical *kenōsis* that seems to be both secular and antireligious. Martin Luther's own conception of eucharistic presence falls between the poles marked out by de Man and Derrida, while bearing a family resemblance to some basic impulses in Benjamin and Derrida that reflect their Jewish roots.

The last part of this chapter examines de Man's later focus on the violent, positing power of language through a close reading of his essay on Percy Bysshe Shelley's poem *The Triumph of Life*. I will suggest that the absence of any promise-fulfillment sensibility in de Man (already discussed in chapter 1) is related to the ethical questions provoked by his reading of Shelley's poem. By privileging rhetoric as a system of epistemological tropes over rhetoric as a means of persuasion, de Man refuses to accept the interdependence of intention and action that lies at the basis of moral character. De Man wants to avoid idolatry, but the absence of meaning that is the cost of that denial seems unavoidably connected with a certain sort of violence. Christian theologians who also want to reject idolatry will need to avoid what de Man claims are the ethical pitfalls of an incarnationalist aesthetic while at the same time escaping the disfiguring violence of language's self-deconstructing subversion of that aesthetic.

Luther on Eucharistic Performance

In his definitive *Confession Concerning Christ's Supper*, Martin Luther analyzes Jesus' words at the Last Supper, "Take, eat, this is my body."[3] Luther argues that these words have two important functions: they denote a certain relation between the eucharistic bread and the body of Christ, and they themselves, as words, bear their own relation to the bread-become-body. The first relation between bread and body is the subject of Luther's discussion of the function of the word *is* in the statement "This is my body" and is the main point of his dispute with Ulrich Zwingli and John Oecolampadius over the nature of a trope. The second relation, between the words and the bread-become-body, is the subject of Luther's resistance to Zwingli's separation of the imperative and descriptive portions of the words of institution. Zwingli wants to detach the imperative "Take, eat" from the declarative "this is my body." Luther insists that the statement must be taken as a whole and that priority must be given to its imperative aspect. He argues that when understood this way, the entire utterance becomes performative—as much a deed as a word.

Luther contends that the statement "This is my body" is not a trope of any sort. It is not analogous to the statement "Christ is a flower," which Luther, perhaps recalling a line from a popular hymn, uses to illustrate the kind of trope found in the Bible. In biblical tropes, the sequence is always "Christ is an *x*," where *x* is a trope for Christ. But in the words of institution, the sequence is reversed and thereby decisively altered: bread (and not just any *x*) is the body of Christ. In the tropological statement "Christ is a flower," flower is a trope for Christ, but in the eucharistic words, the bread *is* Christ—it is not a trope *for* Christ. Likewise, Christ cannot be a trope for bread (for, as Luther insists, Christ is never a trope at all; rather, all biblical tropes are tropes for Christ). Luther appeals at this point to Augustine's operative distinction between signs and things: Christ is always a thing, never a sign.

Nevertheless, Luther does use the tropological statement "Christ is a flower" in order to illuminate the nontropological character of the statement "This is my body." The comparison proves illuminating not because the first statement is tropological, but because of the force of the word *is* as it appears in both statements. Luther insists that even in a tropological remark, *is* always means "is" and never means "represents." The result is not to make "this is my body" tropological, but to regard even a mere tropological remark like "Christ is a flower" as though it were a quasi sacrament; that is, in the tropological remark, Christ really *is* in some sense a flower (although—and this qualification is vital—we are also told that for this to be the case, *flower* must become essentially a new word). How much more, then, in the nontropological remark, is bread really Christ. Luther's comparison makes even biblical tropes for Christ a matter of greater similarity than one might imagine if one understood *is* to mean "represents."

If "this is my body" is not tropological, what sort of utterance is it? Luther says it is the *most literal* utterance one could imagine. On the other hand, he also says that bread is not similar to the body of Christ; one can, he says, scarcely imagine two more different entities. This striking formulation deserves some reflection. Luther is talking about a kind of utterance that posits identity but is not dependent on a natural similarity between signifier and signified. He is describing a oneness that is not a simple, univocal being based on a shared natural essence or substance. This most literal of utterances contains both radical identification (like de Man's symbol) and radical difference (like de Man's allegory). Luther's literalism consequently embraces more than de Man's reductive hypertextuality. Luther's interpretation replicates with respect to the eucharistic bread precisely the point made about the person of Christ in the Chalcedonian Creed: the human nature neither *is* nor *represents* the divine nature, nor vice versa; rather, human nature and divine nature come together in one person without divergence or mixture.[4] This formulation of a christological identity that is built upon difference is ultimately rooted in a conception of trinitarian unity-in-difference.

Luther's application of the Chalcedonian rules to the understanding of the Eucharist necessarily leads him to reject Zwingli's trope of *alloeosis* ("exchange" or the "turning of one thing into another"). It is important to recognize at the outset that Luther is not defending a particular view of language in his debate with Zwingli; indeed, Zwingli may offer a much more plausible account of how human language customarily works. Instead, Luther wants to bend human language to serve his doctrinal ends; he is worried about how to speak properly (that is, with theological correctness) about what he regards as the central mystery of the Christian faith. He wants human language and human reason to serve the divine mystery, and he thinks that Zwingli has done the opposite.

Luther argues that Zwingli's *alloeosis* must be rejected because it overturns the central rule of the Chalcedonian Creed (Christ is one person in two natures) by dissolving the personal union and attributing Christ's actions not to the person but to the natures as Zwingli's understanding of human and divine natures would require. For example, since divine nature cannot suffer, Jesus must have suffered only in his human nature. Zwingli admits that one can use different forms of speech in speaking of this suffering, but they are to be understood as forms of speech that do not correspond to reality. Zwingli can say, then, that only Christ's human nature suffered on the cross (versus Luther's insistence that Christ suffered *according to* the human nature). Zwingli's figure of *alloeosis* allows him to speak not of the personal union but of "the interchange [*de alloeosibus*] of the two natures in Christ, by which in naming one nature we mean the other, or name them both but mean only one." Zwingli's "interchange" is diametrically opposed to the Christian concept of *communicatio idiomatum* (sharing of attributes), which insists that, with respect to the figure of Christ, whatever can be properly predicated of God must be predicable not of one nature or the other but of the human person. Zwingli effectively subverts the notion of the *communicatio* since, by means of his exchange, one could "name both natures" but mean only one, or attribute something to one nature but not to the other. Thus Luther observes that by *alloeosis*, Zwingli can argue (as does Ludwig Feuerbach, following similar assumptions) that the phrase "the Word became flesh" could be rephrased as "flesh became the Word," or "Man became God."[5] In short, then, *alloeosis* dissolves the hypostatic union affirmed by the Creed of Chalcedon, as Luther was quick to point out in the course of defending the appropriateness of saying that God really suffered and died on the cross:

> Now if the old witch, Lady Reason, alloeosis' grandmother, should say that the Deity surely cannot suffer and die, then you must answer and say: That is true, but since the divinity and humanity are one person in Christ, the Scriptures ascribe to the divinity, because of this personal union, all that happens to humanity, and vice versa. And in reality it is so. Indeed, you must say that the person (pointing to Christ) suffers, and dies. But this person is truly God, and therefore it is correct to say: the Son of God suffers. Although, so to speak, the one part (namely, the divinity) does not suffer [here Luther agrees with Zwingli that the divine nature, apart from the hypostatic union, cannot suffer], nevertheless the person, who is God, suffers in the other part (namely, in the humanity).[6]

Luther concludes that Zwingli "fashions his own tropes to pervert Scripture and divide the person of Christ, as he has also done with the word 'is.'"[7]

Luther calls his own Chalcedonian position, as formulated against Zwingli, a synecdoche. He gives as an example "Christ died according to his humanity." Here Luther is following a common medieval scholastic usage of the formulation *secundum quod est* or "according to." Luther's synecdoche differs from *alloeosis*, which would make his example read: "Christ's human nature died." Luther's use of the term *synecdoche* must also be carefully distinguished from de Man's. For de Man, the term indicates a relation of a part to a whole that comprehends that part in a larger unity. But the Chalcedonian Creed, though referring to the two natures of one Christ, does not permit those natures to be regarded as parts of a larger whole; rather than placed side by side, so to speak, the two natures might be imagined as superimposed, producing a unity that nonetheless does not deny the distinction of superimposed natures. But even as we imagine this, we must remember that imagination itself, as a mode of spatialized thinking, constantly forces one to use synecdoches even when trying to overcome them. By synecdoche, then, Luther does not denote a part-to-whole relationship but merely indicates that what Zwingli seeks to separate should remain together. *Synecdoche* for Luther is a term that, by condensing a Chalcedonian rule, preserves what in de Man's terms would be a tension between symbol and allegory, or between synecdoche and metaphor: the radically disjunctive allegory/metaphor pole rules out any natural presence of the divine, while the radically unitive symbol/synecdoche pole insists on some form of real presence. Luther summarizes his view, concluding with a direct quotation of the Chalcedonian Creed:

> They raise a hue and cry against us, saying that we mingle the two natures into one essence. This is not true. We do not say that divinity is humanity, or that the divine nature is the human nature, which would be confusing the natures into one essence. Rather, we merge the two distinct natures into one single person, and say: God is man and man is God. We in turn raise a hue and cry against them for separating the person of Christ as though there were two persons. If Zwingli's alloeosis stands, then Christ will have to be two persons, one a divine and the other a human person, since Zwingli applies all the texts concerning the passion only to the human nature and completely excludes them from the divine nature. But if the works are divided and separated, the person will also have to be separated, since all the doing and suffering are not ascribed to natures but to persons. It is the person who does and suffers everything, the one thing according to this nature and the other thing according to the other nature, all of which scholars know perfectly well. Therefore we regard our Lord Christ as God and man in one person, "neither confusing the natures nor dividing the person."[8]

Luther also wants to stress the performative character of the words of institution. He denies Zwingli's separation of the words of institution into imperatives and indicatives; Luther insists that "this is my body" follows upon, and is subordinate to, the larger imperative context in which it occurs—"*Take, eat,* this is my body." Luther argues that the imperative opening governs the whole utterance, which, as the command of Christ, is divine and consequently has the performative force of God's utterance in Genesis, "Let there be sun and moon." As divine deeds, the divine words of God and Christ enact the realities they describe. Luther offers Baptism as a further illustration. When the priest says, "I baptize you," what is indicated is simultaneously accomplished because the priest's indicative statement is in fact embraced and determined by Christ's command to "Go ye therefore and baptize." As a result, in the eucharistic words, "everything that the words declare does take place, by the power of the divine imperative through which they are spoken."[9] As Luther explains further:

> Here, too, if I were to say over all the bread there is, "This is the body of Christ," nothing would happen, but when we follow his institution and

command in the Supper and say, "This is my body," then it is his body, not because of our speaking or our declarative word, but because of his command in which he has told us so to speak and to do and has attached his own command and deed to our speaking.[10]

The power of the sacrament resides, then, not in the faith of those who participate, but in the truth of God's word and command.[11] Likewise, its power does not depend on the communicant's ability to perceive or to understand the mode of divine presence that it affords:

> We know perfectly well that, to judge by our sight, what is here below cannot be above, and vice versa; for this is a human, visible mode of existence. But God's Word and works do not proceed according to our eyesight, but in a way incomprehensible to all reason and even to the angels. So Christ is neither in heaven nor in the Supper in a visible manner, nor as fleshly eyes judge a thing to be at this place or that.[12]

Yet while the communicant is not required—indeed, he or she will always be unable—to comprehend *how* Christ is present in the Eucharist, the positive spiritual efficacy of the sacrament for any particular individual does require his or her faith *that* Christ is present; divine performance makes the deity powerfully present, but human faith is needed for that presence to be efficacious for the believer. "In the Supper," Luther says, we have not "the fact" of the passion and forgiveness of sins but "the application" of it.[13] Luther underlines the distinction between the sacrament's power as divine performance and the role of the participant's faith: "a bodily eating without spirit and faith is poison and death."[14] The divine performance, not the human act of faith or spiritual perception, ensures that when the minister utters the words "this is my body," the eucharistic bread is Christ's body since the actual speaker in the performative sense is Christ.

Luther's notion of divine performance intersects with de Man's explicit and provocative dismissal in "The Rhetoric of Temporality" of the possibility that a divine will might generate a form of language that was simultaneously symbolic and allegorical. After contrasting the temporally cognizant allegory with the time-denying, spatially dependent symbol, de Man rules out a mode that would somehow combine the two in a single figure:

> The secularized thought of the pre-romantic period no longer allows a transcendence of the antinomies between the created world and the act of creation by means of a positive recourse to the notion of divine will; the failure of the attempt to conceive of a language that would be symbolical as well as allegorical, the suppression, in the allegory, of the analogical and anagogical levels, is one of the ways in which this impossibility becomes manifest.[15]

Is the conceptual impossibility de Man describes here similar to the one created by Luther's insistence on the nontropological understanding of the words of institution, "this is my body"? To the extent that those words are a symbolic utterance, they would stress similarity between the bread and Christ's body; to the extent they are allegorical, they would stress the difference. The statement asserts that bread is, and does not merely represent, the body of Christ. Mere representation comes close to what de Man calls allegory, but the kind of connection being marked by the term *is* surely is not the symbolic one that de Man rejects. Instead, Luther's *is* denotes a relation that "transcends the antinomies" represented by allegory and symbol. Transcendence of these antinomies requires moving to a different category altogether—that of performance. Later in this chapter we will see that de Man has his own conception of performance, one much darker than Luther's.

De Man on Benjamin's Pure Language

Luther's understanding of the words of institution can be related further to de Man's practice of deconstructive reading by way of de Man's remarks on an influential essay by the Jewish literary critic Walter Benjamin. Benjamin's essay is entitled "Die Aufgabe des Übersetzers," which might be translated either as "The Task of the Translator" or "The Failure"—or perhaps "The Giving Up"—"of the Translator."[16] I suggest one think about the utterance that Luther regards as the most literal ("this is my body") as analogous to Benjamin's notion of a pure language toward which all translation gestures, a language of pure literality in which there would be no disjunction between words and meanings. Perhaps such a language would also be analogous to the "impossible space" that de Man identifies as the impossible combination of symbol and allegory.

For Benjamin, pure language is denoted by that "mode of signification" in the original text that the translation replicates in its own language. In order to begin to relate Luther's understanding of the literalism of the eucharistic words to this idea of pure language, we might consider the statement "this [bread] is my body," as spoken by Christ, to be analogous to the statement "This [translation of the *Iliad*] is my *Iliad*," as spoken by Homer. We might ask: To what extent or in what way does the bread "translate" the body of Christ? At least one obvious shared idea endorses the analogy I am proposing: just as Luther wholly rejects the meaning "represents" for "is" in the words of institution, so does Benjamin reject the notion of translation as a representation of the original's meaning. Instead, for Benjamin, translation is said to bear some relation to a pure language that consists of maximal literalness because it lacks the distinction between word and meaning.

In his remarks on Benjamin's essay, de Man gives special attention to Benjamin's analogy of the broken vessel.[17] Benjamin uses the image of a vessel broken into fragments in order to describe the relation between an original text and its translation. Benjamin's analogy, in Harry Zohn's translation (the accuracy of which de Man disputes), goes as follows:

> Fragments of a vessel which are to be *glued together* must *match one another* in the smallest details, although they need not be like one another. In the same way a translation, instead of resembling the meaning of the original, must lovingly and in detail incorporate the original's mode of signification, thus making both the original and the translation recognizable as fragments of a greater language, just as *fragments are part of a vessel*.[18]

Following Carol Jacobs, de Man rightly observes that Zohn's translation misleads in several ways.[19] Benjamin does not say that the fragments "match" one another but rather "follow" one another (*einander zu folgen*); he does not say that they are to be "glued" together but rather are to be "articulated" together (*um sich zusammenfügen zu lassen*); and finally, he does not say that "the fragments are *parts* of a vessel" but rather that they are "the *broken part* of a vessel" (*Scherben als Bruchstück eines Gefässes*). According to Jacob's translation, what Benjamin actually wrote was more like this:

> Just as fragments of a vessel, in order to be *articulated* together, must *follow* one another in the smallest detail but need not resemble one another, so, instead of making itself similar to the meaning [*Sinn*] of the original, the translation must rather, lovingly and in detail, in its own language, form itself according to the manner of meaning [*Art des Meinens*] of the original, to make both recognizable as the *broken part* of the greater language, just as fragments are the *broken part* of a vessel.[20]

By replacing the metonymic notions of articulation, following, and brokenness with the metaphoric notions of gluing, matching, and unbroken parts of greater wholes, Zohn has, according to de Man, illegitimately given us a Benjamin who invokes versions of synecdoche to account for the way translation and original come together as parts of the larger totality of pure language. De Man contends that such a notion does not represent Benjamin's real intention, which is to undercut precisely such a "religious statement about the fundamental unity of language."[21]

Given the inherent ambiguities of Benjamin's own account of the vessel, it is important to grasp the particular way in which de Man has chosen to imagine Benjamin's illustration. De Man imagines a fragmented vessel that, when whole, represents pure language. He first thinks of one fragment of the vessel as the original text. He then imagines a fragment within that

fragment and thinks of it as the translation. The resulting chain of fragments is altogether synecdochic: the translation is a fragment of another
fragment (the original), which is itself a fragment of the larger whole (pure
language). De Man then resists this possible interpretation by drawing on
his translation of the singular *Bruchstück* as the plural "broken parts," which
he thinks implies an endless series of fragmentation:

> The translation is a fragment of a fragment, is breaking the fragment—so
> the vessel keeps breaking, constantly—and never reconstitutes it; there
> was no vessel in the first place, or we have no knowledge of this vessel, or
> no awareness, no access to it, so for all intents and purposes there has
> never been one.[22]

De Man's quick move from fragments as the "broken parts" to the claim
that the vessel constituted by those fragments has never existed involves a
considerable departure from what Benjamin's text seems to say. Replacement of the phrase "fragments are a part of a vessel" with "fragments are
the *broken* parts of a vessel" does indeed get rid of the suggestion that the
translation is a part of a larger whole that is the original. When Benjamin
writes *"broken* part," he intends, I think, to keep the parts separated from
one another, and does not suggest that they break more than once, or keep
on breaking ad infinitum. That a part is *broken* need not mean that the part
is broken in some way beyond its basic and original breaking away. Thus, to
say that a translation is "a fragment of a fragment" does not require us to
infer that it was the act of translation that caused the break; indeed, Benjamin does not discuss the act of breaking at all, but instead draws the
analogy with the presence of an existing breakage. Also, de Man's point
about not reconstituting the vessel seems unwarranted since Benjamin's
account is noteworthy for not addressing either the pre- or the postfrag-
mented vessel; breaking and reconstituting are not his concerns. Instead, he
addresses the peculiar character of the relation of fragments to one another:
they are different in substance and shape yet nevertheless reiterate one
another's contours. Finally, de Man goes much further than anything Benjamin suggests when he insists that lack of knowledge of a prefragmented
vessel is equivalent to there never having been one. For de Man, such
primordial absence of the vessel stands for the sort of absence according to
which nothing has ever been present. But Benjamin has not insisted on
such absence of the unified vessel; he seems more concerned with the peculiar reality of the relation between the contiguous edges that never touch.

In his "Des Tours de Babel," an essay on Benjamin's essay, Jacques
Derrida picks up on this idea of a possible presence "between the gaps"
with his notion of an absence that seems to hint at a prior or potential
presence.[23] Thinking along these lines requires us to reconsider how we are

to imagine Benjamin's illustration in the first place. Derrida's reading of Benjamin's analogy seems to require us to imagine something like this: that both original and translation are fragmented, and that the fragments of the translation reiterate (that is, reenact the fault lines of) the fragments of the original. That is, we must imagine that the edges of the fragments correspond precisely, in their similarities and differences, across the gap that separates them. The gaps between the fragments of the original and the gaps between the fragments of the translation gesture, in their isomorphic lines of separation, at pure language, which, in its purity, would be pure separation, or pure literality without distinction of word and meaning—what Derrida announces as a presence that is present only in the mode of its absence.[24]

There is for Derrida, as for de Man, unquestionably an absence at the heart of Benjamin's vision, but Derrida's absence differs from de Man's. Derrida describes an absence in which a presence is announced or promised, according to an existing contract.[25] Derrida certainly stresses, like de Man, the fragmented character even of the original, using the language of exile: "From the origin of the original to be translated," he writes, "there is fall and exile."[26] But to say that "in the beginning was fall or exile" is altogether different from saying that "in the beginning there was nothing at all." For de Man, what the translation reveals as it replicates the mode of signification of the original is the instability of that mode of signification, its failure to constitute a totality or—and this is the real point of contrast with Derrida—its not being a departure from such a totality, even a departure that might properly be termed an exile. In contrast, for Derrida, Benjamin's exile denotes the primordial disjunction between the fragments of the vessel—the distance between those curvatures and indentations that are precisely one another's complements. This complementary gesture described by Derrida remains anticipatory:

> A translation would not seek to say this or that, to transport this or that content, to communicate such a charge of meaning, but to re-mark the affinity among the languages, to exhibit its own possibility. And that, which holds for the literary text or the sacred text, perhaps defines the very essence of the literary and the sacred, at their common root. I said "re-mark" the affinity among the languages to name the strangeness of an "expression" ("to express the most intimate relation among the languages"), which is neither a simple "presentation" nor simply anything else. In a mode that is solely anticipatory, annunciatory, almost prophetic, translation renders *present* an affinity that is never present in this presentation.[27]

> The sacred and the being-to-be-translated do not lend themselves to thought one without the other. They produce each other at the edge of the same limit.

This kingdom is never reached, touched, trodden by translation. There is something untouchable, and in this sense the reconciliation is only promised. But a promise is not nothing, it is not simply marked by what it lacks to be fulfilled. As a promise, translation is already an event, and the decisive signature of a contract. Whether or not it be honored does not prevent the commitment from taking place and from bequeathing its record.[28]

How might we locate Luther's understanding of "this is my body" as a translation in the midst of these views? De Man's concept of absence, as negation of presence, oscillates on what we might call a spectrum of representation. Consequently, the absence at the heart of translation as de Man has it is not quite relevant to Luther's distinction of bread and body because Luther does not locate that distinction on the spectrum of representation. Even in its most positive meaning, the bread cannot properly be said to represent the body of Christ successfully. Hence, even saying that the body is absent would scarcely confront Luther's claim for the real presence of Christ. In other words, one has to be playing the "representation game" in order for the charge of absence of representation to have meaning, and Luther has refused to play that game.

Luther's formulations are more paradoxical than any representational sensibility allows for:

You must place this existence of Christ, which constitutes him one person with God, far, far beyond things created, as far as God transcends them; and on the other hand, place it as deep in and as near to all created things as God is in them. For he is one indivisible person with God, and wherever God is, he must be also, otherwise our faith is false.[29]

Luther draws on several analogies to help establish the possibility of a real presence of Christ's body in the bread. His analogy of the broken mirror is especially interesting since it seems similar to Benjamin's image of the broken vessel. Luther notes that the image of a face appearing in one intact mirror appears simultaneously in all the fragments of that mirror when it is broken. His point is that Zwingli's assumption that Christ is in heaven and therefore cannot be anywhere else at the same time is false (just because my face is reflected in a single mirror does not mean that it cannot be reflected in many mirrors at the same time, even though the mirrors—in this case, the fragments of a mirror—occupy different spaces).[30] But it is important to note what Luther's analogy is not designed to show: it is not designed to stress the similarity between the original and its many reflections. Rather, the analogy is presented for the highly circumscribed point of illustrating the performative capacity of the deity to make itself present in many places at once, not to represent itself. Had Luther been interested in representation, one might have expected him to talk about the similarity, or even equivalence, between the image in the unbroken mirror and its reflections in the fragments, or between all of the faces and the single face that they reflect.

Luther's conception of the various modes of divine presence is firmly rooted in divine acts of self-instantiation, which can occur in three different modes. The one person of Christ assumed the first mode in the ordinary life of Jesus and in his postresurrection appearances to others, and he will also appear in that form on the last day when he returns. He manifested himself in the second mode when his resurrected body passed through stone and wood. And he presents himself in the third mode as an act of God: "because God and man were one person," "Christ . . . acquired a supernatural mode of existence or mode of being whereby he can be every-where."[31]

These modes are directly correlated with various degrees of human spiritual perception. The first, corporeal mode is what unaided human reason or the "fleshly" understanding can perceive, before the new birth.[32] Reason's understanding is always synecdochal: "Of course, our reason takes a foolish attitude, since it is accustomed to understanding the word 'in' only in a physical, circumscribed sense like straw in a sack and bread in a basket. Consequently, when it hears that God is in this or that object, it always thinks of the straw-sack and the breadbasket."[33] The second, spiritual mode requires faith in order to be perceived.[34] This mode is now common to angels and devils, and will be common to the saints in heaven.[35] This is also the mode of presence in the Eucharist. Luther offers as analogies vision in air, light, water; sound in air, water, walls; light and heat in air, water, glass, crystals: "Therefore he [Christ] must be in the Godhead in a greater and more profound manner than he is in the stone or the door, just as he is in the stone and the door more intimately and profoundly than in his clothes or in the open air."[36] In the third, divine mode, Christ's body is one person with God:

> My friend, whether the humanity is in one place or in all places, it does not enclose the divinity; much less did the stone, which was in one place, enclose his body. Rather, it is one person with God, so that wherever God is, there also is the man; what God does, the man also is said to do, what the man suffers, God also is said to suffer.[37]

Luther's thinking about eucharistic presence is intimately related to his teaching on justification: *simul iustus et peccator* ("at once both a righteous person and a sinner") points to a paradox, not a constructed synthesis that de Man might deconstruct. Luther's notion of faith, as contrasted with the scholastic emphasis on infused love, underscores the peculiar character of the presence of Christ as the object of faith:

Therefore Christian faith is not an idle quality or an empty husk in the heart, which may exist in a state of mortal sin until love comes along to make it alive. But if it is true faith, it is a sure trust and firm acceptance in the heart. It takes hold of Christ in such a way that Christ is the object of faith, or rather not the object but, so to speak, the One who is present in the faith itself. Thus faith is a sort of knowledge or darkness that nothing can see. Yet the Christ of whom faith takes hold is sitting in this darkness as God sat in the midst of darkness on Sinai and in the temple. Therefore our "formal righteousness" is not a love that informs faith; but it is faith itself, a cloud in our hearts, that is, trust in a thing we do not see, in Christ, who is present especially when He cannot be seen.

Therefore faith justifies because it takes hold of and possesses this treasure, the present Christ. But how He is present—this is beyond our thought; for there is darkness, as I have said.[38]

Coleridge is a much easier target than Luther for de Man's subversive deconstruction because Coleridge, despite the Chalcedonian rules that inform his understanding, defines the literary symbol in contrast to allegory in ways that make it difficult for his language to resist de Man's reading. The specific term in Coleridge's account that, according to de Man, betrays his own intention is *translucence,* a term that seemingly overprivileges dissimilarity when read alongside notions of organic substantiality that apparently overprivilege similarity.[39] With terms like these, Coleridge can easily be read as having taken a place on the spectrum of representation (or, more accurately, as having failed to protect himself against a misreading that would so locate him); de Man is then able, like an unrelenting Søren Kierkegaard drawing out the implications of the Socratic view in *Philosophical Fragments,* to push Coleridge along that spectrum in the direction of a lack of representation. Without a humanly inconceivable, yet eschatologically intelligible, paradoxical formulation of incarnation in Chalcedonian terms, this sort of movement (which is the same as Zwingli's *alloeosis*) will always be possible. The resulting de Manian *aporia,* marked out by the poles of the representational spectrum, will, then, always be a matter of undecidability or indeterminacy. The *aporia* contrasts directly with the Chalcedonian formulation, a Christian (and not merely conceptual) paradox, whose undecidability by human beings (because of human finitude—and also because it is not essentially an epistemological matter) does not alter its reality as a divine act.[40]

In contrast, Derrida's focus on Benjamin's announced or promised presence, even though that presence is present only in the mode of its absence, comes much closer to Luther's understanding of a bread that is a body while being altogether dissimilar from that body. Nevertheless, Luther speaks of the situation as one of "real presence," while we might term Derrida's one of "real absence" (perhaps in contrast to de Man's "empty

absence"). But Derrida's emphasis on the mode of promise or announcement does pick up something of the performative aspect of Luther's characterization. For Luther, bread is body finally not because a person says it is
so, nor because of any of the specifically linguistic oddities of the manner in
which a person says it is so; instead, bread is body because the divine
performer wills it to be so.

De Man on Shelley's Disfiguration

We have already seen how Bloom's insistence that tropes are simultaneously
rhetorical and psychological brings his notion of poetic originality closer to
Christian revisionary reading than does de Man's reduction of figuration
to pure textuality. Similarly, Derrida's account of Benjamin's "presence in
the mode of absence" opened up by translation seems more like Luther's
notion of real eucharistic presence than does de Man's insistence that translation is antirepresentational. There are, of course, significant differences
between Bloomian and Christian revision, and between Derrida's account
of Benjamin's "pure language" and Christian accounts of eucharistic presence. But even those differences seem to occupy the same "space of questions," a space from which de Man (and de Man's Benjamin) seems to be
absent.

I suspect that Luther is more like the Benjamin of Derrida and less like
the Benjamin of de Man because Luther's promise-fulfillment perspective
resonates with a certain Jewish dimension of Derrida's and Benjamin's
thinking. Likewise, Luther's difference from de Man, like his difference
from Zwingli, reflects in part his resistance to the binary epistemological
oppositions of Greek philosophical categories of thought (for example, representation vs. reality; sign vs. signified) in favor of categories more common to the biblical tradition, such as action, will, and promise. Such
comparisons suggest that de Man's deconstruction may subvert a Greek
philosophical rather than a specifically Christian view of language. If so, de
Man's poststructuralist thought might systematically lead devotees away
from distinctively Christian forms of spirituality and textuality.[41]

Signs that this might be the case appear in "Shelley Disfigured," de
Man's late, powerful essay on Shelley's last poem, *The Triumph of Life*.
There de Man echoes, but also moves beyond, his earlier deconstructive
subversions of synecdoches (his claim that Coleridge's symbol is unwittingly
allegorical, or that Benjamin's "pure language" is not an actual whole of
which originals or translations are parts). He now turns full attention to a
feature of language beyond the merely indeterminate relation of signified to
signifier—the positing power of language, a power that is inescapable and
violent. At this point, one should remember that Jesus' words at the Last

Supper, as words of institution, might also be thought of as words of positing. But the performative utterance of the Christian Eucharist commemorates a passively received violent act through which was enacted nonviolent love; the positing of the eucharistic words as acts of love will need to be distinguished from the irreducibly violent impositions of the textuality that de Man's deconstructive reading reveals.

Shelley wrote *The Triumph of Life* in 1822, and it remained unfinished upon his death at sea. Left in a fragmented state, it has been restored and rearranged by editors, but the text is still marked by various uncertain and missing passages. This poem is regarded by many as the greatest Romantic palinode because of its representation of the failure of Romantic visionary aspiration, as well as its bleak personal testimony to Shelley's despair as poet and person. My brief consideration of de Man's reading of this poem cannot begin to do justice either to the poem's rich subtleties and complexities or to the question of the literary critical adequacy of de Man's response to it. Instead, I aim only to tease out those features of the inner logic of de Man's reading that enable him to find in Shelley's dark insight into the language of poetic imagination a specific illustration of de Man's own more general theoretical claims regarding language—and indeed, reality—as such. A summary of the plot of the poem, while by no means the key to its internal textual dynamics or deep pathos, may nonetheless help orient first-time readers. The dominant image in the poem is that of a triumphal procession: a Roman general, recently returned from his conquest, parades in a horse-drawn chariot before the populace. This image is intertwined with images of ancient Dionysian revelry. The poem's narrator tells of a kind of trance he underwent in a wooded setting as the sun rose. In the trance, he sees the triumphal procession and inquires about the chariot and the shape within it. In response to an inquiry by the narrator, the voice of Rousseau answers and recounts the fortunes of his own life. The remainder of the poem consists of Rousseau's account of his life, punctuated by questions from the narrator. The text ends in midsentence, cut off by the poet's untimely death.

In his analysis of this poem, de Man rejects the key category that animates Bloom's thought. Central to Bloom's poetics is the presumption of a relationship, one in which every poet finds himself or herself locked in a struggle to the death with a poetic precursor. De Man raises the possibility of relationship, only to reject it. He opens his discussion of the poem by using its unfinished character as a way of questioning the category of relation. One form relationship might take is temporal: one might conceive of a relation between a past and a present, and then, as an archaeological endeavor, seek to deduce the past from the present to which it bears some essential relation. Or relationship might take a spatial, synecdochic form, joining a fragment to something whole, such as Shelley's fragmentary poem to the whole poem he might have written, or Romanticism to some larger movement of which we regard ourselves as participants. De Man observes that Shelley's poem itself thematizes the issue of relationship by having first the narrator, and then the narrator and Rousseau, probe the possible connections between their present and earlier selves. De Man announces that, following Shelley, he too will press the question of "the possibility of establishing a relationship to Shelley and to romanticism in general,"[42] precisely by probing the reader's relation as reader both to the fragmentary poem and finally to Shelley himself. "What relationship," de Man asks, "do we have to such a text that allows us to call it a fragment that we are then entitled to reconstruct, to identify, and implicitly complete?" What have we done, de Man asks by the essay's end, with the dead Shelley?[43]

What readers of de Man's essay discover they have done to the fragment of Shelley's poem, to Shelley himself, and finally even to Romanticism, is to impose tropes of self-mystifying and self-serving continuity on language's own violent, discontinuous acts of imposition. As readers of texts, persons, or cultural moments, we seek to evade the violent acts performed by language itself by means of what we (falsely) regard as our own nonviolent imposition of tropological unities. In so doing we deceive ourselves in two ways: these acts of tropological imposition are not ours but those of language itself, and such acts could never be nonviolent. De Man argues that the actual disfiguring death of Shelley that abruptly truncates his poem produces a "mutilated textual model" that "exposes the wound of a fracture that lies hidden in all texts."[44] This fracture challenges all readers of the poem, forcing them to ask how they are to "dispose of Shelley's body." Shelley drowned when his boat capsized. His decomposing corpse was burned on the beach when it washed ashore some time later (except for the heart, which would not burn and eventually was returned to Mary Shelley). When de Man writes that readers of Shelley's poem are led to ask themselves how they will "dispose of Shelley's body" (now inhabiting the margins of his truncated poem), he is, in part, asking whether readers will acknowledge or repress the horrific story of the disposition of Shelley's actual body—whether their acts of reading will or will not turn into yet another aestheticizing effort to ignore the specificity of that body and what it suggests about the failure of poetic vision. In de Man's words, Shelley's "mutilated textual model" asks readers how they are to read "the textuality" of the "sequence of symbolic interruptions" in the poem that are themselves repetitions of the same disfiguring death suffered by their author.[45]

De Man's essay is, then, about the kind of reading that Shelley's poem calls forth because of the functions of language that the poem itself enacts. The kind of reading it properly and inevitably calls for, "reading as disfigu-

ration,"[46] stands opposed to the kind of reading it more typically elicits—
"monumentalization," a futile, self-mystifying evasion of disfiguration.
Monumentalization (synonymous in this essay with recuperation, historicism, and historical archaeology) involves turning Shelley's dead body (and
his poem) into a "historical and aesthetic object." Its key element is the
evasion of the text's power by means of the reader's cognition based on a
perception of unity or continuity between knower and known, a knowledge
and a value that one might then praise or condemn: readers fool themselves
into thinking that they discern a line of continuity, which only serves to
mask their own present state of deficiency. Such a reading is a recuperation
of what is missing by appealing to an other to which one bears some sort of
natural relation.

But, de Man warns, it would be naive to assume that such continuities
actually exist in the poem. On the contrary, Shelley's poem warns that there
are no relationships in reality, only random occurrences, and that our own
efforts to evade this chaotic circumstance by the imposition of pseudoconti-
nuities, despite recognition of their fictionality, is inevitable.[47] De Man
suggests, then, that "reading as disfiguration" involves a double recognition—of what language does and of what it does to itself in the guise of our
own linguistic efforts at monumentalization or recuperation. In making this
double revelation, reading as disfiguration reveals the mechanism and necessity of our own efforts at recuperation. But the disfiguring reading does
not thereby itself necessarily become recuperative, at least as long as one
allows that reading to act as a kind of prophetic criticism of the customary
and unwitting idolatry of one's language (language idolatrous not because it
fails to serve a god, but because it always serves the self as though the self
were a god).

Such a reading might become recuperative if it sought to postulate theoretically its own superior reliability. But even though "reading as disfiguration" is "historically more reliable" than the recuperative reading it resists,
"to monumentalize this observation into a *method* of reading would be to
regress from the rigor exhibited by Shelley which is exemplary precisely
because it refuses to be generalized into a system."[48] Disfigurative reading
undermines any recourse to system, method, or theory, all of which presuppose the presence of unities and continuities that ground claims to knowledge; instead, it brings one face to face with the dark inevitability of the
slide in all reading, away from any understanding, toward an abyss
of mere repetition, a "madness of words":

. . . to read is to understand, to question, to know, to forget, to erase, to
    deface, to repeat—that is to say, the endless prosopopoeia by which the
    dead are made to have a face and a voice which tells the allegory of their

demise and allows us to apostrophize them in our turn. No degree of
knowledge can ever stop this madness, for it is the madness of words.[49]

De Man's analysis of Shelley's poem is intended to expose the inevitable
slide described above—the "trajectory from erased self-knowledge to disfiguration" that is "the trajectory of *The Triumph of Life*."[50] The principal
scene of "erased self-knowledge" appears in Rousseau's description of his
encounter with the "shape":

> And as a shut lily stricken by the wand
> Of dewy morning's vital alchemy,
>
> "I rose; and, bending at her sweet command,
> Touched with faint lips the [   ] cup she raised,
> And suddenly my brain became as sand
>
> "Where the first wave had more than half erased
> The track of deer on desert Labrador;
> Whilst the [   ] wolf, from which they fled
>   amazed,
>
> "Leaves his stamp visibly upon the shore
> Until the second bursts. . . ." (lines 401–10)[51]

What exactly is erased self-knowledge, what is disfiguration, and how does
Shelley's poem take its readers from the first to the second?

We can begin with the poem's representations of self-knowledge, present
in poetic figures that have a "specular" structure, a structure in which "the
text serves as a mirror of our own knowledge and our knowledge mirrors in
its turn the text's signification."[52] Like a well of water in which one sees
one's reflection, such specular tropes express those notions of identity, unity,
and continuity so dear to the recuperative sensibility. But Shelley's specular
tropes also exhibit a tenuousness that betrays the extreme fragility of self-
knowledge: his specular tropes are "hovering," even though this hovering
may not at first appearance adversely affect the specular understanding that
the trope provides. The key example of such a trope or figure is the rainbow: "Specifically, the figure of the rainbow [Iris in Shelley's poem] is a
figure of the unity of perception and cognition undisturbed by the possibly
disruptive mediation of its own figuration":[53]

> "A Shape all light, which with one hand did fling
> Dew on the earth, as if she were the dawn,
> And the invisible rain did ever sing
>
> "A silver music on the mossy lawn;
> And still before me on the dusky grass,
> Iris her many-coloured scarf had drawn:" (lines 352–57)

Here Iris or the rainbow hovers uneasily between "light" and the "music" that will ultimately constitute the rainbow's "disruptive mediation of its own figuration."

This "disruptive mediation," which signals the erasure of self-knowledge, occurs when the hovering of the specular figure becomes such that the representational feature of the trope collapses (Narcissus plunges into the pool, or the shape that glides upon the waters suddenly plunges beneath the waves). This collapse occurs when music (in the mode of measure rather than the harmony and melody of song) gains the upper hand. De Man offers these formulations on the basis of a close reading of specific shifts in the poem's imagery, such as the contrast between imagery blending song and the natural world ("all the place/Was filled with many sounds *woven into one/Oblivious melody, confusing sense*/Amid the gliding waves and shadows dun") and imagery marking the intrusion of the nonmelodic "articulations" of the shape's feet ("to the ceaseless song/Of leaves and winds and birds and bees/And falling *drops* moved in a *measure new*").[54] De Man writes that "the thematization of language in *The Triumph of Life* occurs at this point, when 'measure' separates from the phenomenal aspects of signification as a specular *representation*, and stresses instead the literal and material aspects of language."[55] By "literal and material aspects of language," de Man means "the accentual or tonal punctuation which is also present in spoken diction"—the "articulation distinctive of verbal sound prior to its signifying function."[56] Here again, we see the way time or temporality disrupts spatial figuration, much the way allegory as the "rhetoric of temporality" undermines the spatialized, synecdochic symbols that would suppress it. We also see de Man's hypertextual sensibility emerge, as his discussion highlights the linguistic functioning of the letter of Shelley's poem in its sheer materiality prior to its signifying function.

Self-knowledge becomes erased when the material or literal articulation by language comes to "extinguish and bury the poetic and philosophical light:"[57]

> "And all the gazer's mind was strewn beneath
> Her feet like embers; and she, thought by thought,
>
> "Trampled its sparks into the dust of death; . . ." (lines 386–88)

One might be tempted to explain this trampling as simply the result of signifiers whose relation to signified meaning has become entirely undetermined. After all, as de Man observes, "the latent polarity implied in all classical theories of the sign allows for the relative independence of the signifier and for its free play in relation to its signifying function."[58] Such free-floating signifiers in the poem might generate their own nonsemantic associations simply by virtue of the interplay of their sound qualities:

If, for instance, compelling rhyme schemes such as "billow," "willow," "pillow" or transformations such as "thread" to "tread" or "seed" to "deed" occur at crucial moments in the text, then the question arises whether these particularly meaningful movements or events are not being generated by random and superficial properties of the signifier rather than by the constraints of meaning. The obliteration of thought by "measure" would then have to be interpreted as the loss of semantic depth and its replacement by what [Stéphane] Mallarmé calls "le hasard infini des conjonctions" (Igitur).[59]

De Man argues that the arbitrariness of the "free play of the signifier" is, by itself, unable to account for the power of this "trampling":

For the arbitrary element in the alignment between meaning and linguistic articulation does not by itself have the power to break down the specular structure which the text erects and then claims to dissolve. It does not account for the final phase of the Narcissus story, as the shape traverses the mirror and goes under, just as the stars are conquered by the sun at the beginning of the poem and the sun then conquered in its turn by the light of the Chariot of Life.[60]

The arbitrary play of signifiers does indeed dissolve or undo the specular, representational, or iconic functions of figures, but does not by itself break them down or bring about disfiguration. This is so because the alignment of signifier with signification is not constitutive of a figure; therefore, mere disalignment does not, by itself, disfigure. A figure as such need not be tied to representative, iconic, aesthetic categories at all; a figure exists only by its creation of "an illusion of meaning." The movements of figures from iconicism to mere matters of the letter (figures of grammar or syntax) prepare the way for, but do not themselves erase, the figure as such: "Another intervention, another aspect of language has to come into play"[61]—the intervention that will account for the trajectory from erased self-knowledge to disfiguration.

De Man spots this intervention in a crucial section of Shelley's poem in which the mysterious shape first glides upon the surface of the water (lines 362–63), becomes subject to the disruption of the measure noted above (lines 369ff.), and then finally "tramples out" the narrator's thought (lines 382–88). The "gliding" is a figure of all figures that are representational— tropological models such as metaphor, synecdoche, metalepsis, or prosopopoeia. Such models always involve a phenomenal element, either spatial or temporal. With the appearance of measure, language continues to articulate meaning, even without representation. Here, figure as representation is displaced by figure as measure (in tropes such as grammar or syntax, "which function on the level of the letter without the intervention of an iconic factor"). But the persistence of meaning despite representation only under-

scores the nonconstitutive role of representation in the production of meaning. Finally, something altogether new intrudes—that other "intervention,"
that other "aspect of language"[62]—erasing the figure, "drowning the shape,"
"trampling out thought."

    In this new intervention, language reveals itself as a violent act of power
(seen from this perspective, the "Triumph" of the poem's title refers not to
the postvictory procession but to the actual victory itself). Now the figure is
seen to be "posited by an arbitrary act of language."[63] By "arbitrary act," de
Man intends a contrast with a "natural event resulting from the mediated
interaction of several powers." Such an arbitrary act is "a single, and therefore violent, act of power achieved by the positional power of language
considered by and in itself."[64] Shelley's awareness of these arbitrary acts
leads him, in the opening lines of the poem, to collapse even "the most
continuous and gradual event in nature, the subtle gradation of the dawn,"
into "the brusque swiftness of a single moment":[65]

> Swift as a spirit hastening to his task
>   . . . the Sun sprang forth
>   . . . and the mask
> Of darkness fell from the awakened Earth. (lines 1–4)

This sunrise is like other events in the poem: not "the natural continuation
of the original, positing gesture but positings in their own right"—they are
consequently "repetitions and not beginnings."[66] De Man characterizes such
repetitions this way:

> The positing power of language is both entirely arbitrary, in having a
> strength that cannot be reduced to necessity, and entirely inexorable in
> that there is no alternative to it. It stands beyond the polarities of chance
> and determination and can therefore not be part of a temporal sequence
> of events. The sequence has to be punctured by acts that cannot be made
> a part of it.[67]

This positing power of language takes de Man further along the path set
out in "The Rhetoric of Temporality." In that essay, time or allegorical
temporality undermined the spatial symbol. Now in the Shelley essay, not
only does time as temporal measure undermine the spatial specular figures,
but the arbitrary imposition of language as sheer act steps outside (and then
"punctures" or, in Shelley's metaphor, "tramples upon") temporally constituted experience as well.

    The later de Man of the Shelley essay has deeply problematized the
relational assumption crucial to Harold Bloom's agon. In a passage that
might be read as almost explicitly written with that struggle in mind, de
Man underscores the utter nonrelationality of Shelley's (and, as is made
clear by the essay's end, his own) view of things, implying that a perspective

see note

like Bloom's, in holding onto an assumption of relation, remains regrettably religious in nature:

> The sun [at the opening of the poem] does not appear in conjunction with or in reaction to the night and the stars, but of its own unrelated power. *The Triumph of Life* differs entirely from such Promethean or titanic myths as Keats's *Hyperion* or even *Paradise Lost* which thrive on the agonistic pathos of dialectical battle. It is unimaginable that Shelley's non-epic, non-religious poem would begin by elegiacally or rebelliously evoking the tragic defeat of the former gods, the stars, at the hands of the sun. The text has no room for the tragedy of defeat or of victory among next-of-kin, or among gods and men. The previous occupants of the narrative space are expelled by decree, by the sheer power of utterance, and consequently at once forgotten. In the vocabulary of the poem, it occurs by *imposition* (l. 20), the emphatic mode of positing.[68]

This act of imposition, unrelated to anything before and after, nevertheless is turned by recuperative readers into a trope that gives rise to "the narrative sequence of an allegory" that is what we regard as the followable narrative of *The Triumph of Life*.[69]

To what would such an allegorical narrative refer? Just what is *The Triumph of Life* about? De Man's reading shows that the poem is about the acts of positing by which its own existence (and its own appearance as being about something) is constituted. Why have readers refused to read Shelley's despairing account of visionary failure honestly? How did we come to think that the poem was about something other (something more reassuring, something less threatening) than its own self-constitution as disfiguration? How did we turn the text as positional act into the text as easily readable narrative? Only by our own (violent) act of imposition—of imposing "on the senseless power of positional language the authority of sense and of meaning."[70] Because even Shelley could not avoid such a recuperative tendency (though it was his courage to refuse to evade his recognition of it), *The Triumph of Life* performs its own "imposition of meaning . . . in the form of the questions that served as point of departure for the reading."[71] But like our own imposition of meaning as readers, Shelley's imposition of meaning as questioning proves illusory: although language posits, and although language means (since it articulates, even when it does not represent), language cannot posit meaning:

> [Language] can only reiterate (or reflect) it [i.e., meaning] in its reconfirmed falsehood. Nor does the knowledge of this impossibility [for language to posit meaning] make it [language's positing of meaning] less impossible. This impossible positing [of meaning] is precisely the figure, the trope, metaphor as a violent—and not as a dark—light, a deadly Apollo.[72]

A trope is the impossible imposition of meaning (hence the "illusior
meaning" noted earlier), taking in this text the form of the all-too-hui
questions posed by the poem's narrator.

The trope is both an initial imposition by language (but only in the f
of repetition, not a beginning) and a subsequent imposition by us
meaning (although even our imposition of meaning is in fact our own
getting" of the prior imposition by language itself):

> To question is to forget. Considered performatively, [our own act d
> figuration (as question) performs the erasure of the positing powe
> of language [through our imposition of "an articulated language of cogni-
> tion"]. In *The Triumph of Life*, this happens when a positional speech act
> is represented as what it resembles least of all, a sunrise.[73]

Forgetting is an ongoing process that is never complete because our own act
of mitigating the violent force of language's own positing by means of
recuperative troping necessarily shares in that violence. Like Rousseau, we
gain power for our words as acts only by relinquishing intention or control
over them:

> For the initial violence of position [e.g., the tracks of the wolf] can only be
> half erased, since the erasure is accomplished by a device of language [by
> our tropes of forgetting, such as "the gradual" sunrise] that never ceases
> to partake of the very violence against which it is directed.[74]

Why does our recuperative trope of the gradual sunrise share in the
violence of the linguistically posited abrupt sunrise? De Man says: "At its
apparent beginning as well as at its apparent end, thought (i.e., figuration)
forgets what it thinks and cannot do otherwise if it is to maintain itself."[75]
Here it is useful to recall once again Nietzsche's essay "On Truth and
Lies." We think about the leaves we see only by the forcible abstraction of
the concept *leaf* from the unique sensory perceptions of individual leaves.
We thereby think the concept *leaf* that bears no resemblance to the actual,
real-life leaves that we think we are thinking about—those actual leaves, one
might say, are forgotten in the very moment of cognition.

As readers of Shelley's poem, we are faced with a double act of language
called disfiguration, the second moment of which misleadingly appears to
us as our own act: "The repetitive erasures by which language performs the
erasure of its own positions can be called disfiguration."[76] De Man here
indicates that both the positing and the erasure of positing by the imposition of meaning are acts of language. "Positing," says de Man, "'glimmers'
into a glimmering knowledge that acts out the *aporias* of signification and of
performance."[77] Our awareness of this *aporia* is an awareness of a perpetual
and undecidable struggle within language itself between language's violent
positing power (performance) and language's forgetting of that positing

power (by imposing signification). There is no reconciliation of these two dimensions of language, but rather an irresolution between them, in which we are implicated. We seek to shield ourselves from awareness of this situation, as does Shelley's poem by allowing the light imagery to persist throughout the narrative. Shelley thereby

> creates the illusion of a continuity and makes the knowledge of its interruption serve as a ruse to efface its actual occurrence. The poem is sheltered from the performance of disfiguration by the power of its negative knowledge. But this knowledge is powerless to prevent what now functions as the decisive textual articulation: its reduction to the status of a fragment brought about by the actual death and subsequent disfigurement of Shelley's body. . . .[78]

The hyperliteralistic notion of textuality that de Man finds illustrated in Shelley's poem seeks to erase all connections with a knowledge or meaning that might be present to the text, or which the reading of a text might make present to a reader. His rejection of presence has an obvious ascetic, religious cast to it: presence is a kind of seduction or temptation, which the lucid reader must renounce or sacrifice.[79] It is, in short, simply a false view of reality, and anyone taken in by it will lead a life of self-mystification, of blindness. To recognize this truth is to gain a kind of sober lucidity or insight into one's inevitable state—and the inevitable but always futile means that one will use to try to evade that state. De Man rather explicitly links the state of blindness or self-mystification (as in the effort to mask the shape's violent trampling out of the sparks of thought with tropes of continuity such as the persistence of light imagery throughout the poem) to an aesthetic perspective that is, in his view, a self-mystifying appropriation of an incarnationalist sensibility.

De Man never reckons directly with classical theological formulations of that sensibility, remaining content to do battle with its Romantic surrogate. Our earlier discussion of Luther's understanding of the real presence of Christ in the Eucharist should have made it clear that the Romantic interpretation of incarnation, controlled by idealist assumptions, is quite removed from classical Christian formulations, guided as they have been by Nicene trinitarian and Chalcedonian christological rules. The target of de Man's critical deconstruction, then, can be seen as a rather serious misconstrual of classical Christian reflection on texts and presence. Consequently, although one might want to accept de Man's criticism of the aesthetic surrogates for incarnation, it would be a mistake to apply that criticism to the classical Christian formulations on which those surrogates are based.

Classical Christianity simply does not rely on the category of representation, which de Man is devoted to undermining. Rather than representation,

Christianity has recourse to a provisional paradox, but de Man cannot seem to entertain the category of paradox at all. Instead, he reads potentially paradoxical formulations as aporetic: where Christians see the presently productive (but only eschatologically intelligible) superimposition of seeming irreconcilables, de Man sees only an undecidable alternation between irreconcilables across an unbridgeable gap—an anti-incarnational void, the "gap that cleaves Being."[80]

Despite talk of gaps that suggests an essentially dualistic vision, de Man replaces all paradoxes with *aporia* because his vision is finally monistic: though it can allow for two oscillating perspectives on the same thing, it can tolerate no true doubleness. De Man's hypertextualist perspective regards texts as finally unidimensional, and any hint of doubleness (a meaning that is not a performance; a performance that is not a meaning) is always judged illusory. De Man's notion of textuality obliterates any dualism in language that would make a place for meaning. What remains is the text's own trampling over those who mistakenly think that they use language to mean, rather than recognizing that they are used by language.

In contrast to *aporia,* paradox is committed simultaneously to unity and distinction. A merely conceptual paradox (a round square, for example) demands acknowledgment of both when it asks us to think an impossible combination. In contrast, Christian paradoxes (a God who became a human being) subordinates our inability to think certain combinations to faith declarations that the divine actions that produced them actually occurred. In contrast to both notions of paradox, an *aporia* gives us two merely apparent incompatibles: it does not demand that we think them both at once, but instead makes one a version of the other—as we saw de Man reduce language as performance to language as epistemological assertion.

De Man's actual reduction to monism, when combined with a specious but insistent commitment to distinction, necessarily leads to violence. The monist insists that since everything is, at some basic level, an instance of the same, wherever two instances of the same seem not to be in the same space (as Aristotle says they cannot be: a thing cannot be and not be in the same place at the same time), there is a problem. When they cannot occupy the same space, and yet, since they are versions of the same thing, are equally entitled to that space, they will compete for it—and such competition will generate a continual violence. De Man's reduction of language to epistemology in the essay on Nietzsche leads inexorably to the violent positing power of language in the essay on Shelley.

In its turn toward disfiguring violence, de Man's language also shares Bloom's assumption of relationship, despite de Man's disavowal of that assumption. Similarly, Bloom's interpoetic agon or struggle, because it is actually the attempt to overcome any valuable duality that relationship might presuppose, shares de Man's assumption of monism: what the ephebe really seeks is the other's annihilation. So while de Man simply drops the category of relation only to have it reappear in the violence necessary to maintaining a monistic vision, Bloom presupposes relation only to turn its violent obliteration into an equally monistic poetic ideal.[81] The fact that it is spirit rather than textuality that has become monistic for Bloom does not change the basic situation; Bloom's monism, like de Man's, endures only by violent means:

> If the imagination's gift comes necessarily from the perversity of the spirit, then the living labyrinth of literature is built upon the ruin of every impulse most generous in us. So apparently it is and must be—we are wrong to have founded a humanism directly upon literature itself, and the phrase "humane letters" is an oxymoron. A humanism might still be founded upon a completer *study of literature* than we have yet achieved, but never upon literature itself, or any idealized mirroring of its implicit categories. The strong imagination comes to its painful birth through savagery and misrepresentation. The only humane virtue we can hope to teach through a more advanced study of literature than we have now is the social virtue of detachment from one's own imagination, recognizing always that such detachment made absolute destroys any individual imagination.[82]

One might think that religion could "found a humanism" where literature fails. But the only religion Bloom can admire is a gnostic faith that is yet another mode of the revisionary poetic imagination, with all of the latter's social failings:

> The religion of the spark or pneumatic self consistently leads to a denial of communal concern, and so perhaps to an exploitation of the helpless by the elite. I want to believe that last sentence of cause-and-effect to be a fiction also, but it is a persuasive fiction, and makes me very unhappy.
>
> The God of the American Religion is not a creator-God, because the American never *was* created, and so the American has at least part of the God within herself. Freedom for an American . . . means two things: being free of the Creation, and being free of the presence of other humans.[83]

For both Bloom and de Man, what is other (the other poet as precursor, or present meaning as the other dimension of textuality) appears as threat or seduction; the threatening or seductive other can be overcome only through violence, in the form of misreading or deconstruction.

The convergence between Bloom's and de Man's sensibilities finds fitting figuration when Bloom's archetypal strong poet, Milton's Satan, pays the price of "being free of the Creation" with a disfigurement that he can discern in his fallen compatriots, but not in himself.[84] Here is the discerning Satan to Beelzebub:

> If thou beest hee; But O how fall'n! how chang'd
> From him, who in the happy Realms of Light
> Cloth'd with transcendent brightness didst outshine
> Myriads though bright. . . . (*Paradise Lost* 1.84–87)

Later, a less discerning Satan on himself:

> . . . Hail horrors, hail
> Infernal world, and thou profoundest Hell
> Receive thy new Possessor: One who brings
> A mind not to be chang'd by Place or Time.
> The mind is its own place, and in itself
> Can make a Heav'n of Hell, a Hell of Heav'n.
> What matter where, if I be still the same. . . .
> > (*Paradise Lost* 1.250–56)

Of course, if Satan remains discerning throughout—if, as Bloom insists, Satan's nobility lies precisely in his courage to go on despite recognition of his altered state—then these lines can be turned against me, standing for Bloom's anti-incarnational rejection of my reading. After all, it hardly matters whether one is disfigured or defaced if one's disembodied mind or spirit can nonetheless persist because it truly is "its own place."

In contrast to the hyperspiritual and hypertextual monisms of Bloom and de Man, the classic Christian theological tradition has insisted on the unity-in-difference of an incarnationalist sensibility, a conceptuality rather rigorously regulated by rules formulated in the christological and trinitarian creeds. Indeed, trinitarian formulations offer the most direct challenge to the monisms of these two literary theorists. Trinitarian reflection, in which the peaceful unity of the deity is enacted precisely via differences that constitute and complement rather than undermine one another, stands in sharp contrast to de Man's and Bloom's monisms that trade on violence. Christian trinitarian reflection insists there can be a kind of unity based on a relation among differences that does not reduce those differences "to mere instances of a common essence or genus." It insists on "a likeness that only maintains itself through the differences, and not despite nor in addition to them,"[85] in contrast to Bloom's would-be poet, for whom "initial love for the precursor's poetry is transformed rapidly enough into revisionary strife, without which individuation is not possible."[86] John Milbank raises some crucial questions in the passage from which I have been quoting for those who promote various postmodern monisms:

> Now, quite clearly we do not live in a world where differences just lie benignly alongside each other, without mutual interference, but, rather, every difference is in itself an "overlap," a disturbance within some area of common space. Yet does one need to interpret every disturbance, every event, as an event of war? Only, I would argue, if one has transcendentally understood all differences as negatively related, if, in other words, one has

allowed a dialectical element to intrude into one's differential philosophy. If one makes no such presupposition, then it would be possible to understand the act of affirmative difference, in its passing over to the other, as an invitation to the other to embrace this difference because of its objective desirability. At the same time, it would have to be admitted that the reception of this difference by the other itself effects a further displacement, a further differentiation. The "commonness" which now embraces them is not the commonplace of the given neutral terrain, nor of the act in its initial conception, but instead of the new differential relationship. The question of the possibility of living together in mutual agreement, and the question of whether there can be a charitable act, therefore turn out to be conjointly the question of whether there can be an "analogy" or a "common measure" between differences which does not reduce differences to mere instances of a common essence or genus. In other words a likeness that only maintains itself through the differences, and not despite nor in addition to them.[87]

Bloom and de Man see differences as only negatively related; Christian theology, in both its christological and trinitarian doctrinal formulations, directly challenges that vision. For Christians, a resistance to idolatry that entails the absence of love is no virtue.

Bloom's and de Man's perceptions of differences as only negatively related reflect their shared opposition to the literary equivalents of idols. Yet each opposes his idol in a very different fashion, and Bloom's opposition makes him a bit less susceptible than is de Man to the criticism I have been advancing. De Man's opposition seems entirely negative or negating: one strives not to be taken in by the false god of apparently present meaning— not because there is a true god that deserves one's regard, but because it is an inherently good thing to be the kind of person who is not duped. In contrast, Bloom always underscores the ambivalent injunction that undergirds the second commandment's prohibition: "Be like me. But do not presume to be too much like me." The first part of this has no correlate in de Man.

Bloom remarks that "though Plato tries to move the trope from Homer's figures of will to a figure of knowing [which is just what de Man does, in Bloom's view], rhetoric remains incurably poetic, a drive toward will-to-identity rather than toward a knower/known dualism."[88] With the phrase "will-to-identity," Bloom formulates part of the biblical deity's injunction ("be like me") and implicitly contrasts it with the only superficially similar "you [as subject] know me [as object]." Bloom shares with de Man the sense that Romantic imagination must be an "idol-smashing" faculty, refusing illusory identifications or shared being between the self and the not-self.

But the idol-making power of the human imagination is not, for Bloom, essentially negating. He locates the motive force of poetry not in a de Manian drive to renounce, but rather in "an energy that in itself is the antithesis of renunciation."[89] Bloom regards de Manian renunciation as an overreading of the second half of the biblical injunction ("do not be too much like me"), an overreading that neglects the first half ("be like me"). Poetry, for Bloom, is the wish for more life, not less. That life seems much the sort that Nietzsche celebrates—a life of ceaseless, vigorous struggle rather than condescending, morally superior pity. But Christian love is neither agonistic nor (as Nietzsche thought) simply a kind of pity. Nietzsche displays a weak understanding of Christian love when he confuses it with pity, but speaks with theological insight when he remarks that the reverence (not contempt!) that the noble feels for his enemy is a bridge to genuine love of neighbor.[90] In that insight lies hidden the potentially productive struggle between Bloom's revision and Christian revision, neither of which, like de Man's deconstruction, seems willing to trade life for the assurance of never being taken in.

But de Man still presents his own challenge for theology: Is not the inability to think, or even to imagine, the unity-in-difference that theology demands prima facie evidence of its fundamental incoherence? Is not the appeal to paradox a sign of this incoherence, simply dignifying it with a technical term? And—perhaps most tellingly—does not appeal to paradox finally suggest that the unity-in-difference not only has been neither thought nor imagined, but has not even been encountered or felt? De Man has been regarded as one who knew at first hand the peculiar temptations of which he wrote (and the revelations about his wartime journalism may lend even more authority to the observation): "The one who has not been tempted would not have spoken so often about the necessity (and the impossibility) of renunciation—and could not have done so with such authority."[91] Thus de Man might want to ask the theologian: Despite your claim to loathe idolatry, have you really felt the seduction I describe? Despite your claim to renounce self for others, have you really attained the rigors of renunciation I describe? Or, while you speak of unity-in-difference, do you really think, imagine, and feel only unity—or, perhaps worse yet, only difference? Are unreconstructed expressivism and ascetic a/theology the only really authentic theologies left for you?

A Christian theologian who hopes to resist reductive, nonincarnational theologies of pure unity or pure difference, having heard and felt Bloom's and de Man's challenges, had better be able to specify the ways in which their critiques of the literary surrogates of the Christian theological tradition are, at least if aimed at classical Christian theology, ever so slightly—and ever so decisively—off the mark. One would do well to take up this task with more than a little fear and trembling: because Christian theologians are prone to drift off their own marks, even the misdirected criticism of these theorists all too often hits home.

3

Body and Consummation

Through his reflections on the authoring of novels, the Russian theorist Mikhail Bakhtin constructs an aesthetic perspective that strives to hold together in creative tension a Bloomian spirit of revision and a de Manian resistance to the presence of meaning on the one hand, while insisting on interpersonal charity and the divine fulfillment of creation on the other. Bakhtin's perspective differs from Bloom's and de Man's formulations by focusing on human embodiment, which Bakhtin regards as more fundamental than either spirit or text. By invoking aesthetic categories of embodiment that find their analogues in religious conceptions, Bakhtin tries to move beyond epistemological accounts of blindness and insight and volitional accounts of interpoetic struggle. To Bakhtin, epistemological and volitional literary categories are equally reductive and monological; both collapse the self-other distinction that is central to both an aesthetic and a religious imagination.

Bakhtin's integrative approach represents an alternative to two main patterns of Western Christian thought, the unitive and the disjunctive. The early Friedrich Schleiermacher is an influential representative of the unitive pattern, Søren Kierkegaard of the disjunctive. The unitive pattern is based on some notion of an essence or being that human beings share with one another and with the deity. The disjunctive pattern insists on radical distinction between human beings and between human beings and God. Resisting this sort of polar opposition, Bakhtin insists that the deepest sort of communality leads to, even as it is constituted by, the heightened distinctiveness and irreducibility of individual persons. Drawing on the Russian Orthodox tradition of a kenotic Christology that stresses the self-emptying of God into the body of Christ, Bakhtin emphasizes notions of communality and interpersonal ethical responsibility that are lacking in much of the

Western liberal tradition. But because his appropriation of the Orthodox tradition is critical in ways that echo prominent Western ideals of human individuality and freedom (ideals rather underrepresented in the Orthodox religious tradition), he is also able to criticize the coercive potential of tradition itself (a self-critical perspective often lacking in some contemporary Western communitarian theories).[1]

The following two sections of this chapter examine how Bakhtin's conception of the ways a novelist "authors" a hero resembles classical Christian reflection on the relation between human self-assertion and divine providence. I outline some influential Christian reflections on the paradox of a divine agency that constitutes rather than subverts genuine human agency. I then explore how Bakhtin conceives of the novelist as one who authors a genuinely free human character. In his thinking on the general issue of how one who authors other persons is able both to free those persons for autonomous agency while simultaneously bringing them to satisfying consummations that they cannot acheive on their own, Bakhtin rejects both a monological, unitive appeal to some form of shared being and a disjunctive insistence on absolute difference. The option Bakhtin develops—the notion of rythmicization—is ultimately grounded in classic Eastern Orthodox conceptions of God's self-embodiment through self-kenosis.

In the next section of the chapter, I show how Bakhtin's transcendence of individual-community oppositions tries nevertheless to do justice to some of the deeply felt, existential insights that animate Bloom's and de Man's projects. Like Bloom and de Man, Bakhtin strives to preserve the individual's freedom, but he wants to avoid Bloom's hyperspiritualist emphasis on a disembodied self and de Man's more radical, hypertextualist disembodiment of the spirit to the point of its elimination. In contrast to Bloom and de Man, Bakhtin strives to make communality humanly productive.

Bakhtin's synthetic vision comes with a cost that some theologians and theorists may judge to be too high, however. In the final section of the chapter, I examine Bakhtin's apparent unwillingness to imagine a genuinely evil or malevolent other—a person who does not complete another person but uses, or even tries to destroy, him or her. Literary theorists schooled in the poetics of resistance or the rhetoric of renunciation may worry about Bakhtin's seemingly overconfident faith in a fulfilling consummation, which looks suspiciously like a recuperative effort to evade all the hard, sharp edges of human existence. And Christian theologians may worry that Bakhtin has not reckoned sufficiently with human sinfulnesss and the apparent intransigence of evil.

This chapter has several more general goals. I hope to introduce readers to the somewhat unfamiliar Bakhtin. Bakhtin's later works on the novel, especially on Fyodor Dostoyevsky and François Rabelais, have attracted considerable attention in the West in recent years, especially among those concerned with literary theory and cultural criticism. Well-known concepts of Bakhtin's such as *heteroglossia* and *carnivalization* have found especially receptive audiences. Much lesser known, because only recently translated into English, are Bakhtin's earliest writings from the 1920s, which probe the relation between aesthetics and ethics. Two such early works will be central for this chapter: "Author and Hero in Aesthetic Activity" and *Toward a Philosophy of the Act*. These two texts, along with the later and better-known "Discourse in the Novel," not only should prove especially intriguing to theologians and theorists with strong philosophical and ethical interests but should also call into question the common celebration of carnival as the essential Bakhtinian contribution to literary theory.[2]

Because the early Bakhtin wrote within a powerful, late nineteenth- and early twentieth-century Russian tradition of lay religious philosophers and aestheticians, he also represents a possible stance for a public theologian that is not typically found in the contemporary West. The West has increasingly seen a sharp split between ecclesiastical theologians and academic scholars of religion, but Bakhtin offers an illustration of a kind of culturally engaged theological thinking that, while not officially linked with ecclesiastical institutions, nevertheless displays deep appreciation for, and engagement with, the Russian Orthodox theological tradition. In the period from about 1880 to 1920 in Russia, prior to the hegemony of Soviet ideology, Russian intellectuals drew on a wide range of theological and philosophical thought to give expression to their complex understanding of various facets of human culture. Bakhtin's early writings reflect the ferment and innovation of this work of lay theologians and intellectuals, and, as such, he represents a possibility for public theology as yet largely unexplored in the West.

As a theologically engaged freelance intellectual, Bakhtin tried to think through many different areas of human thought in ways consistent with his underlying Christian vision. Pursuing an incarnational vision, he can be said to theologize secular culture, or just as appropriately, to secularize theology.[3] Bakhtin's early works display some preliminary results of thinking through literature theologically and reimagining Christian doctrine in literary categories. Because Bakhtin had already begun to integrate Christian theology and literary theory in his early writings on aesthetics, ethics, philosophy, and literature, my analysis will seek to disentangle and explicate a few important features of a complex, synthetic vision-in-the-making.

Providence and Freedom, Author and Hero

Classical Christianity makes a stongly counterintuitive claim about freely acting human beings and the God who created them and providentially orders their lives: The divine actions of creation and providence (including predestination) do not overturn, but actually constitute and enhance, human freedom. In making this point, theologians argue that one should not imagine the interaction of human self-assertion and divine agency according to the way ordinary physical objects interact. Thomas Aquinas distinguishes between physical things, which "are acted on in the sense that they are directed to an end by another," and human beings, who as "self-determining agents . . . shape themselves to a purpose, in the manner of rational creatures who deliberate and choose by free judgment." Human agents are not simply passive objects of divine manipulation but generate their own self-directed activity. This feature of human nature would seem to make reconciling God's providential activity with human self-assertion even more difficult. Yet however difficult it might be to conceptualize this reconciliation, Aquinas makes it clear that God's providence is not altered or diminished by free human acts: "Yet because the very act of freewill goes back to God as its cause, we strictly infer that whatever men freely do on their own falls under God's Providence."[4]

By "falling under God's Providence," Aquinas means to rule out the notion that human willing and divine willing are separate but complementary causes. He insists instead that God is the complete cause of all human activity—even though divine causality, as first and primary cause, works to constitute human beings as secondary causes in their own right: divine causality imparts to creatures "the dignity of causing."[5] Aquinas consequently rejects the arguments of those who would posit human merit as a cause of God's predestinated grace. Merit cannot be a reason for predestination since it, like everything else, is already included within the predestinating will. Those who think otherwise inappropriately "draw a distinction between what springs from grace and what from freewill, as if the same effect could not come from each." But in fact "what is from freewill and what is from grace are not distinct," just as secondary and first causes produce a single result. Consequently, "what is through freewill is also from predestination."[6]

This account of human self-assertion and divine agency is rooted in the peculiar character of the original divine creative act. God originally constitutes the human creature as a reality that is genuinely independent from the divine being precisely because it is utterly dependent on it. As Karl Rahner puts it: "the radical dependence and the genuine reality of the existent coming from God vary in direct and not in inverse proportion."[7] This situation differs entirely from our experience with the relations between ordinary objects in the world. For example, when I will to raise my arm, the more my arm is dependent on me, the less it differs from me, the less it possesses its own reality and autonomy. But if I become subject to epileptic

seizures, my arms will take on lives of their own, becoming utterly independent of my willing. Rahner notes that in ordinary experience, "the radical
dependence of the effect on the cause and the independence and autonomy
of the effect vary in inverse proportion." But in the relationship between
God and self-asserting human agents, "genuine reality and radical dependence are simply just two sides of one and the same reality, and therefore
they vary in direct and not in inverse proportion":

> We and the existents of our world really and truly are and are different
> from God not in spite of, but because we are established in being by God
> and not by anyone else. Creation is the only and unique and incompar-
> able mode which does not presuppose the other as the possibility of an
> effective movement outwards, but rather creates this other as other by the
> fact that it both retains it as its creation and sets it free in its own
> autonomy, and both in the same proportion.[8]

What is true about the God-human relation by virtue of this unique
creative act is true about that relation at the end of human life as well: The
final end of the human being in the beatific vision, which provides the most
direct relation possible between the human person and God, completes the
constitution of the genuine otherness and reality of the person. The vision
of God, as an oxymoronic "immediate relation" to the divine presence, is
nevertheless mediated by the finite subject whose very personhood is enhanced by the experience: "the finite subject does not disappear in this
most immediate manifestation of God and is not suppressed, but rather it
reaches its fulfillment and hence its fullest autonomy as subject."[9] Human
freedom is constituted precisely by its dependence on the creator; the more
intense the dependence, the more autonomous the agent.

In his early essay "Author and Hero in Aesthetic Activity," Bakhtin
works out a similarly paradoxical account involving the human novelist's
authorship of characters. He describes how an author constructs a character
who is a free, autonomous subject, but who is nevertheless rendered a
consummated or finalized whole or hero, a whole that the character could
not attain on his or her own. The author's consummating vision of the other
provides a justification of the life of the character that is independent of the
meaning for which the character struggles, properly but unsuccessfully,
throughout his or her life.

Bakhtin grounds the distinction between author and hero in the basic
and irreducible bodily distinction between persons. By virtue of a unique
embodiment in a particular space and time, a human being brings to himself or herself, to other persons, and to the surrounding world a perspective
that is at once distinctive, limited, and excessive. It is distinctive simply by
virtue of one's embodied location, which gives one a viewpoint that cannot

be exactly replicated by anyone else. Because this viewpoint is fixed and unique, it is necessarily limited: we cannot see the backs of our heads, or any number of things that are available to the views of others. But our viewpoint is at the same time excessive because we stand in the position of other in relation to those persons around us, and because what is lacking in their perspectives is precisely what is present to our view of them: I can see the back of your head; consequently, your lack of vision is my excess of vision and vice versa. The result is that we need one another if we are to achieve full perspectives.

In novels, the author's excess of vision with respect to the would-be hero provides a completion of the character's life, which the character's own limited perspective could never achieve; characters cannot become the heroes of their own lives. Bakhtin works out this author-hero relationship accord-ing to spatial and temporal categories since it is a person's specific embodi-ment in space and time that creates the opportunity for the excess of seeing. The author completes or consummates the character by bringing the char-acter's "outer body" (the body that the character cannot fully see precisely because of the limiting aspects of his own embodiment) into relation with his "inner body" (his body as experienced internally via physical sensation). And the author also brings the character's soul (the temporal unity and wholeness unavailable to the character in the midst of his daily striving for meaning) into relation with his spirit (the driving inner life force of the character that impels him to surpass his givenness in favor of what is new and therefore potentially more meaningful).

We can examine some of the features of the author-hero relationship and some of the key terms in which Bakhtin imagines it by exploring the phrase *sympathetic coexperiencing*. The author sympathetically coexperiences the life of the character who will become her hero. This process needs to be distinguished from a pure coexperiencing in which the author as person would come to share or replicate the character's life, the hallmark of an expressive aesthetic that Bakhtin opposes. For Bakhtin, such pure coexperi-encing would be inappropriate for the author's aesthetic task as author, for its presence would mean that the author had failed to exploit the value of her position outside the character in favor of a kind of merger. Sympathetic coexperiencing, which Bakhtin regards as a manifestation of love, resists the temptation to merge with the other, instead preserving the aesthetically productive ("form-giving") advantages of outsideness.[10]

By ourselves, we cannot unite our inner striving with our outward bodies as unified acts of being; we require someone to come from outside and provide a point of view that can unite us and make us integral beings. The outsider's view integrates by giving us our necessary form in time and space (which turns our directedness into a direction and our horizon into our environment). Bakhtin argues that the specifically aesthetic gift of those outside us is to unify us temporally and spatially: "a whole, integral human being is the product of the aesthetic, creative point of view and of that point of view alone."[11]

We typically aim either at cognition (our directedness, or the ceaseless striving of our spirits for meaning) or at goodness (our sense of ethical obligation, which is never satisfied); our outer world stretches before us as an ever-receding horizon rather than an encompassing, homelike environment. We are dispersed in both time and space—in permanent free fall or exile, never arriving home, so to speak. The loving outsider's form-giving point of view provides something valuable beyond ("transgredient to") what we can provide for ourselves: "From the very outset, sympathetic co-experiencing introduces values into the co-experienced life that are transgredient to this life; it transposes this life from the very outset into a new value-and-meaning context."[12]

In light of the Christian accounts of human self-assertion and divine agency examined above, what is initially striking in Bakhtin's formulations is that the category of will tends to be attributed to the nonaesthetic life of the would-be hero but not to the aesthetic vision of the author. The character is said to exercise his or her will—to be engaged, for example, in an ethical life of evaluating and choosing—but this is presented as precisely the realm in which the character will not be able to achieve any overall unity and completion to his or her life: "Moral self-reflection knows no given that is positive, no present-on-hand being that is intrinsically valuable, inasmuch as—from the standpoint of that which is yet to be attained (the task to be accomplished)—*any given is always something unworthy*, something that ought not to be."[13]

In contrast, the art of the author in rendering this life complete is not generally discussed in terms of the author's willing; instead, Bakhtin describes the consummating role of the author as the rendering of a form rather than the exercising of a will. This reflects the strong separation that Bakhtin makes between the person in the role of author, and that same person acting not as author but simply as the person she is. As an ordinary person, the author will be engaged in just the sort of unconsummated willing that characterizes her unconsummated characters; but that same person as an author—as she enacts her authorial role—is engaged in a nonethical, aesthetic task—describable in Kantian terms as a purposiveness without purpose. Bakhtin draws similarly strong distinctions between a character in a novel who is a to-be-consummated hero, and that same character as simply one person among others striving for meaning. Such striving on the part of the character-as-person occurs in the realm of free choice and morality: the character's acts of will and his moral reflection on them cannot attain to any satisfying completion; he cannot give up the purposeful inner moral struggle in favor of the purposelessness of aesthetic completion. Such a character's inner determinateness possesses this inner purposelessness "only when it is illuminated *not* by meaning, but by love regardless of any meaning whatsoever." Aesthetic love or aesthetic contemplation "must abstract from the constraining validity of meaning and purpose." In the wake of the consummating vision of the author, "object, meaning, and purpose cease to govern axiologically and turn into mere characteristics of a lived experience as *an intrinsically valuable given.*"[14]

But while I, as a striving individual, cannot see my striving for meaning as anything attained, or realized as essentially mine, my needed consummation also cannot be one that simply disregards my striving for meaning. That sort of inattentive, imposed consummation-as-heteronomy would destroy my distinctively human being. How, then, can the given as unworthy be transformed into an intrinsically valuable given, a givenness that fulfills rather than disregards or subverts my own inner-directed quest for meaning? All the moments of striving that I cannot incorporate into my present being must be "rendered immanent to . . . [my] lived experience." Those moments must be "gathered into a soul that is in principle finite and definitively completed, that is, must be concentrated and enclosed within this soul."[15] Only such a "concentrated soul is capable of becoming an aesthetically valid hero in the world."[16]

In order for all this to happen, I need to assume a position impossible for me: "I must go beyond the bounds of my striving, must take up a position outside it, in order to be able to *see* it in the flesh, i.e., *embodied* in valid inner flesh."[17] Here Bakhtin correlates the notion of vision with that of embodiment, drawing on the Orthodox insistence that spatial disposition is centrally important for proper spiritual orientation.[18] A complete embodiment seems to require a stance from which it can be seen, in such a way that what is inner can achieve integration with, be rendered immanent to, what is outer on the same plane. The same thing is asked of an icon: that it make visually present the embodied *logos*.

There is, of course, a difference between the embodiment that makes me a human being with a body as well as a soul, and the embodiment I need in order to become a consummated human being who is the hero of my life. This second embodiment (or second birth) is a transposition or, better yet, transfiguration—a transformation from embodiment as a category of unredeemed creation to embodiment as a category of a transformed, spiritual creation. Although I have a body by virtue of biological birth, Bakhtin insists that I cannot perform my own needed act of transfiguring embodiment. I need someone else to help me fully embody myself.

This embodying vision of the other is what gives the temporal striving of

my life a fulfilling rhythm: my needed consummation requires that my
spirit's striving not be disregarded but "made immanent to" my embodied
life (comparable ways exist of consummating the spatial dimension of the
hero as well; Bakhtin refers to this as giving form to a person's life by means
of an image). Rhythm is the temporal category in which Bakhtin integrates
the literary equivalents of divine providence and human self-assertion:

> Rhythm presupposes a certain *predeterminedness* of striving, experiencing,
> action (a certain hopelessness with respect to meaning). The actual, fate-
> ful, risk-fraught absolute future is surmounted by rhythm—the very
> boundary between the past and the future (as well as the present, of
> course) is surmounted in favor of the past; the future as the future
> of meaning is dissolved, as it were, in the past and the present—is artisti-
> cally predetermined by them (for the author-contemplator always encom-
> passes the whole temporally, that is, he is always *later,* and not just
> temporally later, but later *in meaning).*[19]

Bakhtin's discussion of the author's introduction of rhythm into the hero's
inner lived life echoes Aquinas's account of providence; both thinkers want
to find a way of representing a genuine striving for a meaning or purpose
that is, seen from a different perspective, already somehow in place. When
Bakhtin says that the author-contemplator is always "later in meaning," he
means that any meaning that the would-be hero might strive for already
awaits him: the author-contemplator is already at the end of the journey
that for the hero-to-be is still under way. Likewise, Aquinas suggests that
the effects or purpose that a person thinks his future actions will bring
about already preexist the person's performance in the atemporal mind of
God:

> Since he [God] is the cause of things through his mind, and, as we have
> already made clear, the idea of each and every effect must pre-exist in
> him, the divine mind must preconceive the whole pattern of things mov-
> ing to their end. This exemplar of things ordained to their purpose is
> exactly what Providence is.[20]

Bakhtin's notion of the author-contemplator as later not only in time but
in meaning is reflected in Aquinas's notion of an exemplar as an idea that is
"always already" present in the deity's atemporal mind. Because Aquinas's
deity is outside time, just as Bakhtin's author "encompasses the whole of
temporality," being "prior" in the divine mind is effectively the same as the
author's existence "later in meaning" (at this point, both thinkers verge
toward a kind of monism—a problem to which I will return in the final
section of this chapter). Aquinas's perspective carries the same implication
as Bakhtin's: there is a "certain hopelessness with respect to meaning" (that
is, one need not fret over attaining ultimate meaning for one's life) since

preexisting ideas make it clear that what human persons achieve or secure by their actions (their "effects") will not attain a meaning that is not "already in place." Hence, insofar as meaning is crucial to human life, it does not depend for its realization on the particular actions of human beings independent of the providential ordering of secondary causes.

The crucial moment at which rhythm becomes relevant is when one is poised on the edge of decision, the point at which being and obligation come into conflict—here all is absolutely unpredetermined with respect to meaning. This is an arhythmic moment, in which rhythm threatens to become "a distortion and a lie."[21] Bakhtin offers the following explication of this moment of crisis, of juxtaposition between the character of one's inner striving and the ordering power of the aesthetically consummating other:

> Free will and self-activity are incompatible with rhythm. A life (lived experience, striving, performed action, thought) that is lived and experienced in the categories of moral freedom and of self-activity cannot be rhythmicized. Freedom and self-activity create rhythm for an existence that is (ethically) unfree and passive. The creator is free and active, whereas that which is created is unfree and passive.[22]

This passage suggests that we can attribute free agency to the author, but not to the hero whom the author has rhythmicized. Bakhtin seems to dissolve the counterintuitive view we saw in the theological accounts, leaving in its place an active cause and passive object. Doing this, according to Aquinas and Rahner, would be to fall into that ordinary, categorical way of thinking in which dependency and autonomy vary in inverse proportion. So far, this passage suggests that the authorial equivalent of providence or grace eviscerates genuine human agency on the part of the consummated hero.

Bakhtin then begins to characterize and qualify the effects of rhythmicization on the would-be hero: "To be sure, the unfreedom, the necessity of a life shaped by rhythm is not a *cruel* necessity, not a necessity that is indifferent to value (cognitive necessity); rather, it is a necessity bestowed as a gift, bestowed by love; it is a beautiful necessity."[23] By saying that rhythmicization is not indifferent to value, Bakhtin suggests that the author's consummating fashioning of the hero connects in some positive way with the hero's own moral striving (that is, the hero's "givenness" is, in fact, seen to have truly intrinsic worth). This would be consistent with the earlier suggestion that rhythm requires a certain "immanentization of meaning," a certain consolidation of meaning and purpose that is adequate to one's striving. The author's creative reaction (or aesthetic love) is one that "produces values that are transgredient in principle to the hero and his life and yet are essentially related to the latter."[24] Viewed in this way, Bakhtin's formulation begins to echo the characteristic Christian insistence that the finite subject is not suppressed by its relation to the deity.[25]

The analogue for this possibility of suppression in Bakhtin's discussion may be found in his rejection of impressive aesthetics, which, unlike expressive aesthetics, "loses not the author, but the hero as an independent, even if passive, moment in the artistic event."[26] In such aesthetics, "the artistic event as a living relationship of two consciousnesses does not exist"—"the artist's act of creation is conceived as a one-sided act confronted not by another *subiectum*, but only by an object, only by material to be worked."[27] Bakhtin rejects such a one-sided view by carefully balancing (on either side of a crucial "yet") the literary equivalents of divine grace and human freedom:

> A rhythmicized existence is "purposive without purpose." A purpose is neither chosen nor deliberated, and there is no responsibility for a purpose; the place occupied by an aesthetically apprehended whole in the open event of unitary and unique being is not deliberated, does not come into play, i.e., the whole is axiologically independent of the perilous future within the event of being—it is justified independently of this future.
>
> Yet it is precisely the choice of purpose, the place within the event of being, for which *moral* self-activity is answerable, and in this respect it is free.[28]

Within one's lived experience, one has moral freedom, the choices that locate one in the event of being. But insofar as one's lived life in that event of being becomes an "aesthetically apprehended whole," precisely to that extent the character of one's life is not the consequence of choices one makes but of a gift one receives, bestowed by the love of one's author. The aesthetically apprehended whole of one's life is devoid of the meaning that had previously been always "out in front" of the person. That meaning has now been rendered immanent to the person's achieved life; accordingly, that life no longer stands in need of meaning or purpose but has become justified independently of meaning.

Justification independent of meaning echoes Aquinas's notion of the end or *telos* to which human beings are fundamentally ordered by divine providence (the goodness God creates in things lies not only in their substance but also in "their being ordained to an end, above all to their final end").[29] Such an end is not a matter of a meaning to be striven for, but a purposiveness already built into the scheme of things. Once again, Bakhtin carefully balances grace and freedom:

> . . . what must be found is that particular position in relation to the hero from which the hero's entire world view—in all its depth, and with all its

rightness or wrongness, its good and evil, impartially—would become merely a moment within the intuitable, concrete *existential* whole of the hero. That is, the author must move the very center of value from the hero's existence as a compelling *task* into his existence as a beautiful *given;* instead of hearing and agreeing with the hero, the author must see all of him in the fullness of the present and admire him as such.

> At the same time, however, the cognitive-ethical validity of the hero's attitude as well as the agreement or disagreement with that attitude *are not lost*—they preserve their significance, except that now they become no more than constituents within the whole of the hero. . . .[30]

We should not conclude too quickly, however, that Bakhtin has put the hero as arhythmical in opposition to the rhythmicizing gaze of the author. One must remember that while another person may author my self, I may also prove to be an author for another self. Rather than thinking of this as one self acting upon another, it is more accurately envisioned as the other enabling one dimension of my self (the spirit or "oughtness") to become integrated with another dimension of my self (the soul or "is-ness"). While *ought* and *is* remain forever divided for me in my own mode of spirit, when I encounter the spirit of the other in the category of otherness, then for that other spirit, my *is* and *ought,* my being and my obligation, "are not severed and are not hostile to each other, but are organically interconnected and exist on one and the same axiological plane." The other's "self-activity," though not heroic for himself as seen by himself, is nonetheless "heroic for me and is graciously cherished by rhythm (for the whole of him may be in the past for me, and I can justifiably free him from the ought-to-be, which confronts only myself, within me myself, as a categorical imperative)."[31]

Bakhtin's reflections suggest that we must consider not only the relation between author and hero, but also the relation between the hero as a possible author and the author, who as person rather than author is a potential hero. Consequently, both unconsummated spirit and spirit consummated by soul are internal to every person as a result of encounter with other persons:

> Rhythm is an embrace and a kiss bestowed upon the axiologically consolidated or "bodied" time of another's mortal life. Where there is rhythm, there are two souls (or, rather, a soul and a spirit)—two self-activities; one of these lives and experiences its own life and has become passive for the other, which actively shapes and sings the first.[32]

Bakhtin's description of one's embodiment by means of the gaze of the other is a literary interpretation of a conception of Christomorphic salvation in which one person, with the aid of another, replicates the movement of incarnation. The self-activity or spirit of the person being saved (by being granted soul by the other) replicates the human nature of Christ, which, in the midst of its own living and experiencing, becomes passive to the shaping force of the person of the *logos*. In the case of Christ, the *logos* provides the single source of agency for his (now hypostatically) united divine and human natures. Such a Christ is a recapitulation of the human person (spirit) who becomes the hero of his or her life through the consummating encounter with an other. Although we cannot be the heroes of our own lives, Christ is uniquely the hero of his own life because, as self-embodying *logos*, he enacts his own needed "immanentization of meaning," which is to say that who he is becomes inseparable from what he does; his abiding identity is embodied in (that is, has become immanent to) the particularity of his striving, by way both of his own hypostatically enacted life as the human Jesus, and by his own encounter with God the Father as other. The trinitarian God is consequently both author (as Father) and hero (as Son) of the divine life, and the divine-human Christ is also both author (as person of the *logos*) and hero (as the human being Jesus of Nazareth) of his own life. What is possible for God *in se* and for God incarnate is analogously possible for a human person, but only as lived in encounter with others and, first of all, in encounter with God. Such is the Bakhtinian interpretation of the Eastern Orthodox notion of Christomorphic divinization.

God incarnate recapitulates the human project by fulfilling Godself in relation to the other; salvation as christologically shaped deification offers the same for human beings, and it is the otherness of God that makes it possible: "What I must be for the other, God is for me."[33] This sentence distills the connection between kenotic incarnation and interpersonal communality (*sobornost*). What the person of the *logos* does by hypostatically uniting the two natures of Christ is what the human other (or novelist) does for the human self (or would-be hero) by means of the author's aesthetic-loving consummating gaze:

> What makes a reaction specifically aesthetic is precisely the fact that it is a reaction to the *whole* of the hero as a human being, a reaction that assembles all of the cognitive-ethical determinations and valuations of the hero and consummates them in the form of a unitary and unique whole that is a concrete, intuitable whole, but also a whole of meaning.[34]

The fact that the author reacts to the hero provides recognition of the hero's freedom, but it is also a productive reaction "that assembles," demonstrating the interpersonal equivalent of divine agency. The result does not override the concrete particularity of the individual—he or she remains a "concrete intuitable whole" (just as the hypostatically united Christ remains concretely human). But the consummating gaze nevertheless renders the whole, concrete person "a whole of meaning" (just as the human Christ is wholly divine).

In the following passage, Bakhtin characterizes the aesthetic, form-giving activity of the author as a two-stage process of descent and ascent: the author must first see the world through the eyes of the would-be hero, and then return, with the insight gained, to a position of outsideness, from which the aestheticizing consummation of the hero can begin. First, the descent to the realm of the hero, in this instance one who suffers:

> The first step in aesthetic activity is my projecting myself into him and experiencing his life from within him. I must experience—come to see and to know—what *he* experiences; I must put myself in *his* place and coincide with him, as it were.[35]

It is as though the author is a kind of god who, in order to comprehend the human situation, must become incarnate as a human being—but in so doing runs the risk of an absolute self-reduction to the level of a mere human being. Such a hyperkenosis would mean that deity (authorship) would be given up for good. To reclaim authorial, consummating capacity, the author must therefore return to her former position outside the hero-to-be, bringing to bear upon the character from that outside perspective her previous knowledge of the character's unconsummated self-striving:

> But in any event my projection of myself into him must be followed by a *return* into myself, a *return* to my own place outside the suffering person. . . . Aesthetic activity proper actually begins at the point when we *return* into ourselves, when we *return* to our own place outside the suffering person, and start to form and consummate the material we derive from projecting ourselves into the other and experiencing him from within himself.[36]

This authorial enactment of Christ's incarnation and resurrection/ascension, which preserves and applies in the second moment the knowledge gained in the first, is, from the point of view of the heroicized character of the novel, the literary equivalent of a Christomorphic salvation.

Were the author to fail to make the second movement—the return to a position of outsideness—she would fail as an author, or, in the Christian theological analogue, Jesus would fail to be the incarnate God, remaining a mere human being. We can see how this analogue might work itself out by exploring further Bakhtin's rejection of an expressive aesthetic in drama, in which an actor would simply coexperience the life of the character. In what follows, I take the liberty of juxtaposing Bakhtin's remarks on actor and spectator with some remarks of my own on Jesus and Peter. In the expressive view, an actor expresses the character's life as the actor's own—and it is "at this point that the spectator as well must merge, by means of the 'expressive' form, with the actor."[37] The spectator would achieve much more of a genuine aesthetic perspective if, as a "naive" spectator, he should suddenly leap across the footlights in order to save the hero from an impending danger that the hero cannot see coming. The naive spectator—like the Peter who opposes Jesus' journey to Jerusalem because of the threat of death (Mark 8:31-35)—is "prepared to utilize the privilege of his own *outside* position by coming to the aid of the hero where the hero himself, from *his* place, was powerless."[38]

Bakhtin notes that the attitude assumed by the naive spectator toward the hero is understandable, but it remains naive and aesthetically inadequate because the spectator's leap across the footlights reveals that he still stands on the hero's own cognitive-ethical plane, not on the aesthetic plane. Peter protests Jesus' journey to Jerusalem because he still regards the Christ as mere human being. The naive spectator's mistake, notes Bakhtin, "consists in his failing to find an equally firm position *outside* the enacted life event as a whole." Instead of assuming that position of outsideness, the naive spectator "took up a position *beside* the hero on one and the same plane of life lived as a unitary and open ethical event, and, in so doing, he ceased to be an author/spectator and abolished the aesthetic event."[39] "Get behind me, Satan!" responds the Christ to Peter (Mark 8:33): "for," he might have added in Bakhtin's words, "the event of lived life as a *whole* is without any ultimate issue out of itself. From within itself, a lived life can express itself in the form of an action, a confession-as-penitence, an outcry"—perhaps an outcry such as "my God, my God, why have you forsaken me?" "Absolution and grace," writes Bakhtin, "descend upon . . . [a lived life] from the Author. An ultimate issue out of itself is not *immanent* to a lived life: it descends upon a life-lived-from-within as a gift from the self-activity of another—from a self-activity that *comes to meet* my life from *outside* its bounds."[40]

Hence (to continue my analogy with Jesus and Peter), the Christ will soon meet his death, and its "ultimate issue" will come only from "the self-activity of another"—of the resurrecting God. Thus is the wholeness of Christ's life ultimately "hid . . . in God" (Col. 3:3). Peter is slow to grasp that the Jesus who is the Christ has been journeying toward Jerusalem from the beginning; Jesus has anticipated "from the very outset the hero's hopelessness [that is, he has anticipated his own hopelessness] with respect to meaning." Peter did not realize that "throughout the entire course of an embodied hero's life, one can hear the tones of a requiem," but for those who recognized the import of the massacre of the innocents, "the requiem tones at the end were already heard in the cradlesong at the beginning."[41]

Mikhail Bakhtin on Bloom and de Man

Bakhtin never read the works of Bloom and de Man. But he did encounter in his own day similar literary theoretical tendencies: an ethical tendency that resonates with aspects of Bloom's theory, and an epistemological tendency that echoes aspects of de Man's. Bakhtin judges these ethical and epistemological tendencies to be nonaesthetic because they are both "monological." For him, a genuinely aesthetic event is always "dialogical": it requires "two participants," two "noncoinciding consciousnesses." Bakhtin first describes the ethical tendency:

> When the hero and the author coincide or when they find themselves standing either next to one another in the face of a value they share or against one another as antagonists, the aesthetic event ends and an *ethical* event begins (polemical tract, manifesto, speech of accusation or of praise and gratitude, invective, confession as a self-accounting, etc.).[42]

The coincidence of hero and author, or their common adherence to a shared value, could well represent the traditional understanding of the Romantic, unitive, idealizing sensibility that Bloom opposes. But when author and hero become antagonists, we are close to Bloom's reconception of that Romantic tradition. Given what he writes here, Bakhtin would regard the conflict of wills between ephebe and precursor as an ethical rather than aesthetic event.

Since there is no precursor for de Man, but only a reader confronting the rhetoricity of language itself, there is no struggle between persons (or between poets in persons). Instead, there is simply an ever-present epistemological question: Will the reader be seduced by language's apparent offer of extralinguistic meaning? Or will the reader renounce this temptation in favor of a lucid recognition of the absence of meaning? Bakhtin describes such an epistemological alternative as the reduction of aesthetics to epistemology: "When there is no hero at all, not even in a potential form, then we have to do with an event that is *cognitive* (treatise, article, lecture)."[43]

Against the ethical and epistemological alternatives, Bakhtin presents his own aesthetic understanding of an author's relation to the hero:

> An author is the uniquely active form-giving energy that is manifested not in a psychologically conceived consciousness, but in a durably valid cultural product, and his active, productive reaction is manifested in the structures it generates—in the structure of the active vision of a hero as a definite whole, in the structure of his image, in the rhythm of disclosing him, in the structure of intonating, and in the selection of meaning-bearing features.[44]

Bakhtin's description focuses on the outwardly visible, objective effects of an author's performance: a "durably valid cultural product" consisting of structures comprised of various discernible literary forms. In contrast to Bakhtin's attention to the concreteness of a literary product existing in space, Bloom and de Man focus exclusively on time: Bloom's misreading is a "lie against time"; de Man's deconstruction is a "rhetoric of temporality." For the hyperspiritualist Bloom and the hypertextualist de Man, space in its concrete, material, three-dimensional character, to the extent it figures in their theories at all, is a space to be escaped: it is Bloom's fallen cosmos of necessity, de Man's synecdochic temptation of essential meaning. We can crystallize the contrast with Bakhtin by focusing on the notion of *topos*. For de Man, a *topos* is a conceptual moment in which something is unknown; for Bloom, it is a volitional moment in which something is willed. But for Bakhtin, a *topos* is first of all an actual place in the physical world where one is uniquely and unavoidably situated because one is embodied.

Taking as utterly fundamental the uniqueness of individuals that is a consequence of their embodiments, Bakhtin strives to render productive each person's "outsideness" to other persons. Consequently, he strongly resists any notion of merger or union between persons that would overcome their unique identities:

> The productiveness of the event of a life does not consist in the merging of all into one. On the contrary, it consists in the intensification of one's own *outsideness* with respect to others, one's own *distinctness* from others: it consists in fully exploiting the privilege of one's own unique place outside other human beings.[45]

We have already seen that Bloom and de Man also oppose the idea of merger. Bloom's ephebe resists a merger with the poetic precursor (which would be to "join the tradition," as recommended by T. S. Eliot), cultivating instead unrelenting opposition. De Man insists that signifiers never merge, or achieve a synecdochic relation, with any larger meaning, truth, or presence; he counsels instead an ascetic renunciation of all such idolatrous seductions. But cultivating opposition and renouncing merger are radically different from making outsideness productive. Both the poet's resistance to the hegemonic power of the precursor and the lucid reader's steadfastness in the face of epistemological temptation represent simple, polar rejections of merger. But Bakhtin regards polar rejections of merger as parasitic on the merger theories they resist. Polar opposition turns out to be every bit as monological as direct merger.

Bakhtin works out his critique of monological theory further in his essay "Discourse in the Novel." There he presents what he calls the poetic word (interpreted as trope or symbol) as the paradigmatic instance of monological discourse, in contrast to the distinctive double-voiced quality of the prose word. Bakhtin's distinction between poetic and prose words is not a simple valorization of novels over poems; instead, he is drawing a distinction between two different ways that language functions in both poems and novels: the "prose word" stands for the dialogical function, the "poetic word" interpreted as symbol or trope stands for the monological. The prose word is the clearly valued category, but there are certainly "prosaic" poems whose prosaic quality consists in the authentically dialogical or double-voiced character of the poetry. Bakhtin's notion of the poetic word as symbol/trope is to be understood, then, not as a reference to poetry (note the important qualifying phrase "in the narrow sense" in the passages quoted below), but as an analogue to de Man's notion of the symbol, which, because of its essential, synecdochic link between part and whole, does not place two perspectives in dialogue but collapses meaning and image into a monological unity or merger.

Although the poetic word as symbol/trope, like a prose word and unlike a concept, has more than one meaning, those multiple meanings do not flow from different voices:

> The double-voiced prose word has a double meaning. But the poetic word, in the narrow sense, also has a double, even a multiple, meaning. It is this that basically distinguishes it from the word as concept, or the word as term. The poetic word is a trope, requiring a precise feeling for the two meanings contained in it.
>
> But no matter how one understands the interrelationship of meanings in a poetic symbol (a trope), this interrelationship is never of the dialogic sort; it is impossible under any conditions or at any time to imagine a trope (say, a metaphor) being unfolded into the two exchanges of a dialogue, that is, two meanings parcelled out between two separate voices. For this reason the dual meaning (or multiple meaning) of the symbol never brings in its wake dual accents. On the contrary, one voice, a single-accent system, is fully sufficient to express poetic ambiguity.[46]

Bakhtin sketches out two basic ways one might choose to interpret the relationships between the meanings of the poetic trope or symbol: epistemological and ethical. The former resembles de Man's approach since here Bakhtin invokes de Man's favorite target of synecdoche:

> It is possible to interpret the interrelationships of different meanings in a symbol logically (as the relationship of a part or an individual to the whole, as for example a proper noun that has become a symbol, or the relationship of the concrete to the abstract and so on); one may grasp this relationship philosophically and ontologically as a special kind of representational relationship, or as a relationship between essence and appearance and so forth. . . .[47]

The second, ethical way of handling the symbol's multiple meanings— shifting "into the foreground the emotional and evaluative dimension of such relationship,"[48] resembles Bloom's strategy. Bakhtin argues that both strategies of interpreting the poetic word as symbol fail to attend to the dialogical possibilities latent in the poetic word's doubleness:

. . . these types of relationships between various meanings do not and cannot go beyond the boundaries of the relationship between a word and its object, or the boundaries of various aspects in the object. The entire event is played out between the word and its object; all of the play of the poetic symbol is in that space. A symbol cannot presuppose any fundamental relationship to another's word, to another's voice.[49]

Bakhtin concludes by criticizing the monological solipsism toward which an interpretation of the poetic word-as-symbol or trope verges:

The polysemy of the poetic symbol presupposes the unity of a voice with which it is identical, and it presupposes that such a voice is completely alone within its own discourse. As soon as another's voice, another's accent, the possibility of another's point of view breaks through this play of the symbol, the poetic plane is destroyed and the symbol is translated onto the plane of prose.[50]

Alexander Pushkin's lyrical poem "Parting" provides an example of poetry in which "another's point of view" does "break through"—indeed, Bakhtin's reading of the poem centers on its rendering of the relationship between two persons, and Bakhtin explores how the language of the poem is permeated by the dialogical interchange of their different perspectives on the same event.[51]

Bakhtin links the difference between the genuinely dialogical, double-voiced prose word and the monological poetic word-as-symbol to two fundamentally different notions of linguistic origins, represented by the biblical stories of Adam's name-giving in Eden and the Tower of Babel. The monological poetic word-as-symbol becomes the (futile) quest to recover the lost language of Eden:

In the poetic image narrowly conceived (in the image-as-trope), all activity—the dynamics of the image-as-word—is completely exhausted by the play between the word (with all its aspects) and the object (in all its aspects). The word plunges into the inexhaustible wealth and contradictory multiplicity of the object itself, with its "virginal," still "unuttered" nature; therefore it presumes nothing beyond the borders of its own context (except, of course, what can be found in the treasure-house of language itself). The word forgets that its object has its own history of contradictory acts of verbal recognition, as well as that heteroglossia that is always present in such acts of recognition.[52]

But such a monological possibility is unavailable to any genuinely historical language user, for whom the "heteroglossia," the conflicting voices of many others, will have informed his own recognition and comprehension of the objects he would name. Only the mythical Adam as first name-giver could have such an opportunity to affix original names; only for him would there be no *heteros,* no "other" whose language, already in place, would need to be accommodated:

> Only the mythical Adam, who approached a virginal and as yet verbally unqualified world with the first word, could really have escaped from start to finish this dialogic inter-orientation with the alien word that occurs in the object. Concrete historical human discourse does not have this privilege: it can deviate from such inter-orientation only on a conditional basis and only to a certain degree.[53]

Echoing de Man's objections to Romantic aesthetic ideology, Bakhtin hints further that efforts to recuperate Adamic speech through narrow, monological poetic words-as-symbols contain moments of violence—of breaking through or penetrating a "virginal fullness":

> Even the poetic word (in the narrow sense) must break through to its object, penetrate the alien word in which the object is entangled; it also encounters heteroglot language and must break through in order to create a unity and a pure intentionality (which is neither given nor ready-made). But the trajectory of the poetic word toward its own object and toward the unity of language is a path along which the poetic word is continually encountering someone else's word, and each takes new bearings from the other; the records of the passage remain in the slag of the creative process, which is then cleared away (as scaffolding is cleared away once construction is finished), so that the finished work may rise as unitary speech, one co-extensive with its object, as if it were speech about an "Edenic" world. This single-voiced purity and unqualified directness that intentions possess in poetic discourse so crafted is purchased at the price of a certain conventionality in poetic language.[54]

If Adam as name-giver in Eden stands for the impossible possibility of symbolic language and anti-incarnational evasion of heteroglossia, the Tower of Babel provides a contrasting image of the dialogical prose word incarnated in "heteroglot" language:

> For the writer of artistic prose, on the contrary, the object reveals first of all precisely the socially heteroglot multiplicity of its names, definitions and value judgments. Instead of the virginal fullness and inexhaustibility of the object itself, the prose writer confronts a multitude of routes, roads, and paths that have been laid down in the object by social consciousness. Along with the internal contradictions inside the object itself, the prose writer witnesses as well the unfolding of social heteroglossia *surrounding* the object, the Tower-of-Babel mixing of languages that goes on around any object; the dialectics of the object are interwoven with the social dialogue surrounding it. For the prose writer, the object is a focal point for heteroglot voices among which his own voice must also sound; these voices create the background necessary for his own voice, outside of which

his artistic prose nuances cannot be perceived, and without which they "do not sound."[55]

Bakhtin presents the "prosaic" novel as a kind of necessary antidote (through fostering a Hegelian-like moment of self-recognition) to the linguistic consequences marked by the Tower of Babel, the "failure on the part of those speaking different languages to understand each other":[56]

> In the novel, literary language possesses an organ for perceiving the heterodox nature of its own speech. Heteroglossia-in-itself becomes, in the novel and thanks to the novel, heteroglossia-for-itself: languages are dialogically implicated *in* each other and begin to exist *for* each other (similar to exchanges in a dialogue). It is precisely thanks to the novel that languages are able to illuminate each other mutually; literary language becomes a dialogue of languages that both know about and understand each other.[57]

Bakhtin's notion of the novel as antidote for asocial heteroglossia echoes Augustine's notion of the Bible as antidote to Tower of Babel sinfulness:

> But because vibrations in the air soon pass away and remain no longer than they sound, signs of words have been constructed by means of letters. Thus words are shown to the eyes, not in themselves but through certain signs which stand for them. These signs could not be common to all peoples because of the sin of human dissension which arises when one people seizes the leadership for itself. A sign of this pride is that tower erected in the heavens where impious men deserved that not only their minds but also their voices should be dissonant.
>
> Thus it happened that even the Sacred Scripture, by which so many maladies of the human will are cured, was set forth in one language, but so that it could be spread conveniently through all the world it was scattered far and wide in the various languages of translators that it might be known for the salvation of peoples who desired to find in it nothing more than the thoughts and desires of those who wrote it and through these the will of God, according to which we believe those writers spoke.[58]

For Bakhtin, however, the situation of heteroglossia does not result from a sinful fall, but arises out of entirely natural and irreducible differences among embodied persons. That does not mean that Bakhtin simply collapses a notion of human sinfulness and interpersonal violence into the notion of heteroglossia, as though equating the creation of unique individuals with their fall. Rather, novelistic prose simply chooses to embrace rather than suppress "the historical and social concreteness of living discourse," a discourse "still warm from that historical struggle and hostility, as yet unresolved and still fraught with hostile intentions and accents." It is this raw, unvarnished reality that prose art "subjects . . . to the dynamic-unity of its own style,"[59] much as Augustine's Bible sought to bring linguistic diversity fueled by pride into its therapeutic embrace. Unlike "purely poetic, extra-historical language"—a disincarnate utopian "language of the gods far removed from the petty rounds of everyday life," the prosaic novel is the product of a recognition of the way linguistic diversity, though inescapable, is the condition for its own productive engagement by the novel.

So far we have examined some of Bakhtin's criticisms of the monological limitations of a kind of language he associates with poetic symbols or tropes, one that resembles certain features of Bloom's and de Man's poetics. But Bakhtin also seems to recognize some of the values that Bloom and de Man promote. For example, Bakhtin wants both to acknowledge and modify a view of freedom similar to Bloom's celebration of the originality of the poetic spirit. Bakhtin begins by carefully describing the moment of greatest threat to freedom—the point at which an author begins to bring upon the hero a consummating perspective: "all of the moments that actively consummate the hero render the hero passive, the way a part is passive in relating to the whole which encompasses and consummates it."[60] Here Bakhtin presents passivity as a form of subordination rather than the result of a head-to-head conflict of wills: passivity is described not as the result of one part struggling to displace another, but of the willingness of one part to join others as parts of the whole work. Bakhtin develops this notion of a willing subordination for the sake of a greater whole in the following passage that turns on, while simultaneously easing, the tension between freedom and determinism:

> Form expresses the *author's* self-activity in relation to a hero—in relation to another human being. In this sense, we could say that form is the result of the interaction between hero and author. The hero, however, is passive in this interaction: he is not someone who *expresses*, but someone who *is expressed*.
>
> Yet even as such, he still has a determining effect on the form, inasmuch as the form must answer to *him* specifically, must consummate from outside *his own* inner object-directedness in his lived life, and in this respect, therefore, the form must be adequate to *him*, although not in the least as *his* possible *self*-expression.[61]

In this passage, Bakhtin acknowledges the appropriateness of a Bloom-like aspiration to originality while offering a powerful alternative to Bloom's formulation of that desire. Consummation is a kind of "answering to" or becoming "adequate to" that is not rooted in the Romantic quest for a self-expression, or in a classically unitive hermeneutical bid to think another's thoughts. To be "adequate to" the hero is not the same as to attend to the hero's "possible self-expression." Bloom makes adequacy a matter of authenticity as originality (which would require Bakhtin's hero to declare himself to be underived from his precursors). Such authenticity is indeed a matter of possible self-expression. In contrast, Bakhtin offers an account of the hero's formation by the other that does not need to become a mode of the hero's self-expression in order to be adequate to him. In other words, the hero simply cannot be the measure of his own adequacy, and his self-expression is not the fullest statement of his complete being.

Bakhtin's notion of adequacy bears a striking similarity to the way the edges of the broken pieces of Walter Benjamin's vessel "follow upon" or are "adequate to" one another in such a way as to gesture toward some hypothetically reconstitutable whole. Bakhtin insists that "the hero's inner directedness from within his own lived life possesses its own immanent necessity, its own autonomy,"[62] and it is this paradoxical autonomous necessity to which the form-giving authorship must be adequate. Bakhtin adds that "this inner, immanent necessity of the hero's own object-directed life must be understood and lived through by us in all its compelling force and significance; on this point, 'expressive' theory is in the right." Here Bakhtin endorses Bloom's concern for the subject's expressive freedom. But Bakhtin insists that any such expression "must be understood and lived through in a form which is *transgredient* to that life, i.e., in an aesthetically valid form, which relates to that life not as its *expression*, but as its *consummation*."[63] Transgredience requires otherness, which is precisely what the expressive theories neglect: "Aesthetic form is founded and validated from within the *other*—the author, as the author's *creative* reaction to the hero and his life. As a reaction, that is, which produces values that are transgredient in principle to the hero and his life and yet are essentially related to the latter."[64] The heart of the matter lies in the paradox of a view that is simultaneously transgredient and essentially related to the hero.

Just as Bakhtin both engages and distances himself from features shared with Bloom's poetics, so he engages certain aspects of de Man's theory. If Bakhtin were to criticize the early de Man of "The Rhetoric of Temporality," he might follow at first the lines laid down in Bakhtin's rejection of expressive aesthetics. The kind of heroic freedom implicit in de Man's lucid renunciation of all seductions to meaning would likely be viewed by Bakhtin as one-sidedly inattentive to the way the self is shaped by those outside it, in ways adequate to, rather than subversive of, the self. Although Bloom's hyperspiritualized (and therefore disembodied) self wills to overcome a precursor, and de Man's hypertextualized (and therefore disembodied) "renouncer of seductions" knows in the Socratic sense of being self-aware of his or her lack of knowledge, both conceptions focus on the singular self locked in a polar either-or, a situation in which what proves other to the self can only be threatening or seductive.

One can discern a more subtle relation between Bakhtin and the later de Man of "Shelley Disfigured" on the subject of death, memorialization, and memory. For Bakhtin, death marks the moment at which the author's form-giving capacity to embody or consummate really comes into its own. Upon the death of the other (say, a friend), I need reckon no longer with his continually striving "spirit," for now, "the whole of his life lies directly before me, freed of such constituents as future time, goals, and obligations (the ought-to-be)." After burying my friend and placing a memorial at his grave site, my memory begins to take over in earnest: "I have the other's *entire* life *outside* myself, and it is at this point that the aesthetization of his personality begins: the securing and consummating of his personality in an aesthetically valid image." I am now able to "give form" to my friend's life, drawing upon "the emotional-volitional attitude assumed in commemorating the dead ('remembering the dead in one's prayers')."[65]

In contrast, de Man, focusing on Shelley's disfigured body, can think only of the way burial and memorialization operate as falsifying evasions of the actual identity of the deceased. For de Man, the question of how one "reads the textuality" of Shelley's disfigured poem is the same as the question of how one disposes of Shelley's body. De Man is convinced that readers, unable to bury the real Shelley and unable to read Shelley's poem, have chosen instead to bury Shelley along with "all the other dead bodies that appear in romantic literature" in "their own texts made into epitaphs and monumental graves." The text in which Shelley is buried becomes itself a buried monument, to be uncovered by "future archaeologists"—recuperative readers—who will transform Shelley's text as burial ground and monument into an aesthetic object, the foundation for their own monumentalizing interpretations.[66]

For de Man, the inability to bury Shelley is only evidence of the inability to relate to him; the dispersal that death fully enacts, and the inevitable recuperative or aestheticizing effort to block one's recognition of that dispersal, are both reflections of a world in which the sense of any meaningful relationship can only be the result of a self-mystification:

> *The Triumph of Life* warns us that nothing, whether deed, word, thought, or text, ever happens in relation, positive or negative, to anything that precedes, follows, or exists elsewhere, but only as a random event whose power, like the power of death, is due to the randomness of its occurrence. It also warns us why and how these events then have to be reintegrated in a historical and aesthetic system of recuperation that repeats itself regardless of the exposure of its fallacy.[67]

Although Bakhtin's view of the value of death and the aesthetization it makes possible stands in striking contrast to de Man's vision of random events, Bakhtin acknowledges de Man's (and Shelley's) bleak perception, and makes a place within his vision for it: "Meaning is not born, nor does it die; the meaning-governed sequence or progression of one's life, that is, the cognitive-ethical tension of a lived life from within itself, can be neither started nor consummated." Bakhtin and de Man agree about an essentially meaninglessness dimension of existence. Because meaning can be neither started nor finished, Bakhtin agrees in a sense with de Man that death by itself can bring no meaning forward nor provide any conclusion:

> Death cannot be the consummation of this meaning-governed progression—that is, death cannot assume here the significance of a positive consummation; from within itself, such a progression knows no positive consummation and is incapable of turning back upon itself, in order to coincide contentedly with its own already existent makeup. . . .[68]

Like de Man, Bakhtin acknowledges that death, by itself, reveals more and more of the "rhetoric of temporality" without inner organization, purpose, meaning, or completion.

Yet Bakhtin characteristically incorporates this de Manian recognition within a larger vision of possibility: "a consummation—a consummating acceptance—can descend upon it [the "meaning-governed progression"] only where it is turned to the outside of itself, where, for itself, it does not exist."[69] The very absence that de Man identifies is, for Bakhtin, the condition of a possible moment of transfiguration: only those who lose their lives, says Bakhtin, will find them—they will have them returned to them from the outside. Within there is, as de Man accurately observes, only dispersion and death. Nothing de Man says about the lack of meaningful relation in existence is any less sanguine than what Bakhtin has to say about one's unconsummated state:

> In the dimension of time, on the other hand (if we abstract completely from that which is imposed as a task), I find only my own dispersed directedness, my unrealized desire and striving—the *membra disiecta* of my potential wholeness; whereas that which could assemble these *membra disiecta*, vivify them, and give them a form—namely, their soul, my authentic *I-for-myself*—that is not yet present in being, but is set as a task and is yet-to-be. . . . To *be* for me myself means—to be present to myself as someone-yet-to-be (and *to cease being present to my self as someone-yet-to-be*, to turn out *to be all I can be already here and now*, means—*to die as an intelligent being*).[70]

On the one hand, one's inner-directedness, on its own terms, remains dispersed and unrealized. Yet on the other hand, "to die as an intelligent spirit" (literally, "to die as a spirit") is the high price one pays for keeping oneself open to novelty; one is forced to relinquish one's inner-directedness—a kind of suicidal act (and here the convergence with de Man's Shelley becomes intense) in which one gives up one's unique volitional and cognitive aspirations. The only way out of the struggle between frustrated aspiration and suicidal acquiescence or defiance must be a genuine way *out*—one must be constitutable by someone genuinely outside oneself. Ultimately, however, this outsider must also be the consummate insider: he or she must be able, precisely because of his or her outsideness, to see us from the perspective of our own inevitable deaths. What one needs for one's life is what one can never achieve on one's own: a sense of one's self as one who has finished life, who has died (unable to think our own deaths, we substitute by imagining our reactions to the imagined deaths of those around us). What one needs is an outsider who can bring that retrospective gaze upon us even as we live out our lives. Great novelists can do this for their characters; they can allow readers to see characters freely enact lives that nonetheless express a wholeness that is adequate to them, but which they could never attain on their own: "The aesthetic embodiment of the inner man anticipates from the very outset the hero's hopelessness with respect to meaning."[71]

Evil and the Aesthetic Temptation

In considering the author's creation of a hero, Bakhtin draws on a more general phenomenology of self-other relations. These relations are presented in terms of lack and fulfillment, not in terms of potential opposition or adversarial intent. Bakhtin emphasizes and privileges the potential wholeness and unity of a person's life and the way that "the other" can enable one to attain that desirable state. Interpersonal relations in Bakhtin's vision are largely productive and harmonious. He seems to give little acknowledgment to the various ways that others can impede that quest, or undermine and attack a person; he shows little recognition of the possibility of a genuinely malevolent other.

Bakhtin's apparent inattention to such possibilities has led some literary theorists to criticize him for failing to grasp the tragic side of human existence. Christian theologians may wonder whether Bakhtin has an adequate notion of human sinfulness. Those who have followed my own criticism of monism may wonder whether Bakhtin, despite his professed concern with dialogism, does not verge toward a kind of monism of his own: an aestheticized vision of the world, based not on the contrasts of creator and (fallen) creation but on a vision of a wholly transfigured earth in which the kingdom of God has largely arrived, and in which otherness in creation has assumed the wholly pacific role it has in the Christian view of the Trinity. In short, Christian theologians might wonder whether Bakhtin's vision of reality embraces an overly realized eschatology, and whether his conception of creation is modeled too much in the divine image.

We have partially addressed this question by drawing parallels between Bakhtin's author-hero relation and a God-world (or God-human being) relation. We have already interpreted Bakhtin's aesthetic account of the authoring of a hero as applying not to relations between human beings, but to relations between human beings and God. But in his development of the aesthetic discussion, Bakhtin constantly appeals to a more general phenomenology of persons and interpersonal relations; therefore it is still reasonable to ask whether those accounts attend sufficiently to the question of personal and interpersonal evil.

Although Bakhtin says little directly about such evil in his early essays, one may miss what Bakhtin does have to say about it if one assumes that significant characterizations of interpersonal evil must always take the Augustinian form of a sinful will. One must guard against any tendency to bring to the reading of Bakhtin an overly Western conception of evil, whether in a Christian form supplied by Augustine or in a more secular form supplied by Immanuel Kant. Bakhtin's conception of evil is drawn from the Eastern Christian tradition. For that tradition, death rather than sin gets the most attention as the evil that needs to be eradicated. And Bakhtin gives a great deal of attention to death. Indeed, because he presents death as a great opportunity for fulfillment and final consummation, Bakhtin's discussion takes on the character of a large-scale theodicy. But despite its traditional concern with death, the Eastern Christian tradition still regards death as "the wages of sin," so we still need to ask to what extent Bakhtin is willing to acknowledge that aspect of human existence.

Bakhtin takes up the topic of evil obliquely in *Toward a Philosophy of the Act.* Understanding Bakhtin's thoughts on evil requires one to recognize some basic assumptions he makes about where the roots of evil lie. Those roots lie in the tendency to abstract oneself from life: to gaze over the surface of things and miss their detail, to be indifferent to particulars:

> Lovelessness, indifference, will never be able to generate sufficient power to slow down and *linger intently* over an object, to hold and sculpt every detail and particular in it, however minute. Only love is capable of being aesthetically productive; only in correlation with the loved is fullness of the manifold possible.[72]

What is the cause of such lovelessness and indifference?

The place to begin is with Bakhtin's criticism of aesthetics, historiography, and science insofar as all three are modes of theoreticism by which persons abstract themselves from their own acts of living. Bakhtin writes that "all these activities establish a fundamental split between the content or sense of a given act/activity and the historical actuality of its being, the actual and once-occurrent experiencing of it."[73] This act or once-occurrent experiencing is fully real for Bakhtin only as a realized unity or whole: "only this *whole* act is alive, exists fully and inescapably—comes to be, is accomplished."[74] The problem with the various forms of theoreticism is that each pretends to give an account of this wholeness while remaining abstracted from the "eventness" of the act it seeks to describe:

> The performed act or deed is split into an objective content/sense and a subjective process of performance. Out of the first fragment one creates a single systemic unity of culture that is really splendid in its stringent clarity. Out of the second fragment, if it is not discarded as completely useless . . . one can at best extract and accept a certain aesthetic and theoretical something. . . . But neither in the first world nor in the second is there room for the actual and answerable performance of a deed.[75]

And as a result, two worlds confront each other, two worlds that have absolutely no communication with each other and are mutually impervious: the world of culture and the world of life, the only world in which we create, cognize, contemplate, live our lives and die or—the world in which the acts of our activity are objectified and the world in which these acts actually proceed and are actually accomplished once and only once.[76]

The pernicious split between culture and life results in a disincarnate world of theory that is both unrestricted by and unrelated to the immediacies of life as it is lived:

> The theoretical and aesthetic worlds have been set at liberty, but from within these worlds themselves it is impossible to connect them and bring them into communion with the ultimate unity, i.e., to incarnate them. Since theory has broken away from the actually performed act and develops according to its own immanent law, the performed act itself, having released theory from itself, begins to deteriorate.[77]

How is this unhappy divorce to be overcome? Theoreticism by itself cannot do the job: "all attempts to surmount—from within theoretical cognition—the dualism of cognition and life, the dualism of thought and once-occurrent concrete actuality, are utterly hopeless."[78] Once one has entered into the consequence of theoretical reflection, one has already performed an act of abstraction from one's own individually enacted existence: "the theoretical world is obtained through an essential and fundamental abstraction from the fact of my unique being and from the moral sense of that fact—'as if I did not exist.'"[79]

What seems to be required is a single plane of existence in which theoretical cognition and lived experience might interpenetrate each other— precisely that realm in which, as we have already seen, the author's aestheticizing perspective must become adequate to the striving of the would-be hero as spirit:

An act of our activity, of our actual experiencing, is like a two-faced Janus. It looks in two opposite directions: it looks at the objective unity of a domain of culture and at the never-repeatable uniqueness of actually lived and experienced life. But there is no unitary and unique plane where both faces would mutually determine each other in relation to a single unique unity. It is only the once-occurrent event of Being in the process of actualization that can constitute this unique unity; all that which is theoretical or aesthetic must be determined as a constituent moment in the once-occurrent event of Being, although no longer, of course, in theoretical or aesthetic terms. An act must acquire a single unitary plane to be able to reflect itself in both directions—in its sense or meaning and in its being; it must acquire the unity of two-sided answerability—both for its content (special answerability) and for its Being (moral answerability). And the special answerability, moreover, must be brought into communion with the unitary and unique moral answerability as a constituent moment within it. That is the only way whereby the pernicious non-fusion and non-interpenetration of culture and life could be surmounted.[80]

What is needed, then, is a communion in which a single act can responsibly answer for a theoretical cognition that has become a constituent moment within that act as morally answerable. In other words, when I think my abstract thought, both the content of that thought and my act of thinking it must be integrated into the ongoing act that is my life and for which I am answerable. The temptation is always to fail to integrate the theoretical thought into my life as answerable act, but instead to let it float free—as universally valid or invalid—apart from the individual, historical, concrete, unique act of my life as the one who is thinking just that thought, at just this time, in just these circumstances.

In describing the split between culture and life, theory and experience, Bakhtin is working out the implications of his incarnational perspective. The abstraction that divorces thought from experience opposes an incarnation that would integrate them. The mystery of that "unitary and unique plane where both faces would mutually determine each other in relation to a single unique unity" is a restatement of the internal logic of the Chalcedonian Creed's formulation of the hypostatic union: the two natures of Christ, human and divine, come together and "mutually determine each other" (cf. *communicatio idiomatum* in the glossary under "Hypostatic union").

Bakhtin argues that, on the whole, aesthetics comes closer to integrating theory and life than does either science or historiography. But precisely because of this, aesthetics poses an especially pervasive temptation: it does the best job of presenting the illusion of an achieved integration that it does not, in fact, achieve. In the case of authors and their heroes, the problem goes something like this: As an artist, I can realize an aesthetic whole only for another person. But in doing so, "I shall not find *myself* in that life [that is, in my life-as-artist]; I shall find only a double of myself, only someone pretending to be me."[81] For example, as an author of a novel's hero, my authoring as an aesthetic act requires me to play the role of author vis-à-vis the hero I create and consummate. As an author, I am not equivalent to myself as a person who uniquely and answerably enacts the event of my life; it is not my *playing* the role of author but my *adoption* of that role that is my own answerable act. My role as author is a role I can put on or off: I "assume, like a mask, the flesh of another—of someone deceased."[82] This is only a pseudoincarnation, somewhere between full embodiment and pure abstraction; the real embodiment happens when I *elect* to play the role of author in a particular way:

. . . the aesthetic answerability of the actor and the whole human being for the appropriateness of the role as played remains in actual life, for the playing of a role as a whole is an answerable deed performed by *the one playing,* and not the one presented, i.e., the hero. The entire aesthetic world as a whole is but a moment of Being-as-event, brought rightfully into communion with Being-as-event through an answerable consciousness—through an answerable deed by a participant. Aesthetic reason is a moment in *practical* reason.[83]

In my act of authoring, I am that participant who performs the answerable deed; I am morally answerable for my entire aesthetic act of authoring, apart from the character of the hero I author.

Bakhtin's rejection of the split between theory and life is no simplistic rejection of theory. He recognizes the value and validity of theory, but he also insists that theoretical worlds are not the "once-occurrent world in which I live and in which I answerably perform my deeds"; he observes that "these two worlds [of culture and life] do not intercommunicate; there is no principle for including and actively involving the valid world of theory and of theoreticized culture in the once-occurrent Being-event of life."[84] Neither theoretical cognition nor aesthetic intuition can offer an approach to the "once-occurrent real Being of an event" because both perform an abstraction of content/sense from the act itself.[85]

So far we have seen Bakhtin discuss the perils of theoreticism, including aesthetics. We have seen him distinguish a disincarnate, abstracting act of authoring from the author-as-person's own act of existence. How does Bakhtin integrate into this picture the phenomenon of evil? We can start by observing that he links evil with theoreticism, a link that emerges in a few passing remarks on the perils of technology. Bakhtin declares that technology has pursued the inner aims of its own sense of development apart from consideration of the "cultural purpose of that development." As a result, "it may serve evil rather than good." It is precisely the perfecting of instruments according to their own inner law—a stance obtained by abstracting that development from lived experience—that allowed such technology to develop a "terrifying, deadly, and destructive force." Bakhtin concludes: "All that which is technological, when divorced from the once-occurrent unity of life and surrendered to the will of the law immanent to its development, is frightening; it may from time to time irrupt into this once-occurrent unity as an irresponsibly destructive and terrifying force."[86]

Although Bakhtin's reference to technology does not exactly define evil, it offers a number of clues as to its character. Evil is presented as a possibility that arises when one abstracts oneself from the immediate flux of real life because that abstraction frees up something to proceed according to its own immanent laws in ways that might be fundamentally at odds with the rest of existence from which it has been artificially sundered. This is a vision of evil as a kind of basic disregard for, or inattentiveness to, "the other," where "the other" in question is "the rest of life" from which technology (or theory) has been divorced.

We know that aesthetics, insofar as it is a form of theoreticism, shares the perils of technology to some degree. But we have also been told that aesthetics does a better job of uniting theory with life than do other forms of theoreticism. What is there about aesthetics that allows it to do a better job of incarnating itself in existence and mitigating the evil of abstraction? The key seems to be that the aesthetic vision makes the human person, rather than some abstracted schema, the center of value:

> The unity of the world in aesthetic seeing is not a unity of meaning or sense—not a systematic unity, but a unity that is concretely architectonic: the world is arranged around a concrete value-center, which is seen and loved and thought. What constitutes this center is the human being: everything in this world acquires significance, meaning, and value only in correlation with man—as that which is human. All possible Being and all possible meaning are arranged around the human being as the center and the sole value; everything (and here aesthetic seeing has no bounds) must be correlated with the human being, must become human.[87]

So, presumably unlike the case of technology, art's own immanent laws of development remain tied to its central value-focus on the human. Yet, we have seen Bakhtin resist the notion that this means that the artist in aesthetic creation actually conjoins art and life; the same turns out to be true for the heroes that the author consummates as well. That is, just as the author as author remains distinguishable from his or her act of existence, so does the author's hero as hero. Authorship as an aesthetic event does not tell one anything about the moral character of the author's decision to be an author in this way, and being a hero aesthetically realized by an author is no indicator of the hero's moral act of being a person. Although it is true that the human being is the irreducible center of value in an aesthetic object,

> this does not mean, however, that it is the hero of a work who must be presented as a value that has a positive content, in the sense of attaching some positive valuational epithet to him, such as "good," "beautiful," and the like. On the contrary, the epithets may be all negative, the hero may be bad or pitiful or someone defeated and surpassed in every way. Nevertheless, it is upon him that my *interested* attention is riveted in aesthetic seeing, and everything that constitutes the best with respect to content is disposed around *him*—the bad one—as around the one who, in spite of everything, is the sole center of values.[88]

In this difficult passage, Bakhtin makes a key distinction. Having already insisted that being an author and being that author's hero, as aesthetic events, do not address the moral character of the person who is authoring or of the character being authored, Bakhtin now goes on to describe the particular moral character of the aesthetic act as such. The moral character of that act privileges the goodness of human being, and the moral quality of aesthetic seeing turns on the loving capacity to cherish the human. In a striking formulation, Bakhtin returns implicitly to the author-God parallel we have already developed, suggesting that the artist loves his or her creations the way God loves human beings—not because they are inherently worthy of God's love, but because God's love renders them worthy: "In aesthetic seeing you love a human being not because he is good, but, rather, a human being is good because you love him. This is what constitutes the specific character of aesthetic seeing."[89]

Bakhtin then goes on to work out the aesthetic equivalents of divine mercy and justice. Theologians insist that God's mercy and justice do not conflict: just because God loves human beings without regard to their merit (because of sin, human beings merit only condemnation) does not mean that, in so doing, God becomes oblivious or inattentive to human evil or ceases to judge it. In analogous fashion, just because the artist's aesthetic vision lovingly embraces the humanity of his or her heroes does not mean that a moral assessment of them cannot or should not be made. But it does mean that such moral assessment does not supersede the prior unmerited love of the human:

> . . . aesthetic seeing does not abstract in any way from the possible standpoints of various values; it does not erase the boundary between good and evil, beauty and ugliness, truth and falsehood. Aesthetic seeing knows all these distinctions and finds them in the world contemplated, but these distinctions are not drawn out of it and placed above it as ultimate criteria, as the principle of viewing and forming what is seen;

they remain within that world as constituent moments of its architectonic and are all equally encompassed by an all-accepting loving affirmation of the human being.[90]

Translated back into theological categories, Bakhtin's remarks suggest that while divine mercy does not obliterate divine judgment (that while the value of being divinely created does not mean one can ignore human sin), a priority is given to creation over sin in defining the mainspring of existence. Redemption is clearly conceived as re-creation—or, better, the completing of the creative intention, rather than as the overcoming of an abyss of sin that otherwise fundamentally separates the creature from the creator. In taking this approach, Bakhtin stands squarely in the main current of his own tradition's view of redemption: most Eastern Christianity holds that the image of God in humanity, though defaced by sin, has never been lost, and that the human being, created in the image of God, is consummated or divinized in redemption through the recovery of the fullness of that image. The malevolent other thus finds a place in Bakhtin's vision (hardly a surprise, inasmuch as the censored and exiled Bakhtin encountered more than his share of malevolence). But the malevolent other assumes his or her place within a larger scheme, and, like his or her archetype in Eastern Christianity—Origen's Satan—is given neither the first nor the last word.

Epilogue

The literary theories and Christian theologies discussed in this book offer all-encompassing interpretations of the meaning and significance of human existence. Such has always been the aspiration of Christian theology. That literary theorists have come to offer interpretations of comparable scope is a rather recent phenomenon. In the wake of Christianity's decline in the modern West, the Christian theological reflection that once dominated the intellectual life of "Christendom" (as well as other areas of culture) in the premodern period has given way to surrogate forms of reflection by literary theorists, even as the traditional canon of Scripture has given way to hotly contested modern canons of literary texts, as well as to controversies about the goods and evils of canonization itself.

The three literary theorists I have discussed might well object to my characterization of their works as surrogate theologies, even if they agreed that one can speak meaningfully about a possible nontheistic theology. They might try to restrict the scope of their arguments. Harold Bloom might contend that he speaks only about poets and poetic creation; Paul de Man might contend that he speaks only about language or textuality; Mikhail Bakhtin might protest that he writes only about aesthetics and literature. But, as I hope the preceding pages have indicated, such responses would be unpersuasive. Bloom's view of the experience of poetic creativity simply locates where one needs to look for the most authentic manifestation of the human; de Man's characterization of textuality is all-consuming and, with a reductive rigor, leaves little if any room for other ways of talking about the human condition; and Bakhtin's ruminations on aesthetics draw at every point on sweeping assertions about embodied human life as such. All three theorists offer accounts of the human condition that rival in scope the interpretative aspirations of Christian theologians.

If these literary theorists would likely object to being called theologians, they might just as likely object to being called theorists, if by theory one means an abstract account of something. Bloom insists he is simply a practical critic whose reflections have no point except to help readers read what poets have written; de Man's celebrated defense of theory is in fact a defense of the process of making readers increasingly self-conscious about the intrinsic workings of literature, which their "resistance to theory" helps them evade; and Bakhtin's polemic against theoreticism is an outright rejection of forms of reflection that float above the objects of their attention. Christian theologians would heartily endorse this sort of rejection of theory as abstracted reflection. Like the theorists, they would reject the suggestion that their reflections do anything other than bring readers back to an enhanced encounter with their objects of attention. Indeed, few if any thinkers, either theoretical or theological, have proclaimed that their reflections are anything other than accounts of how things really are; few thinkers have not resisted at every opportunity the charge that their abstract ideas betray the very realities of which they seek to give an account. The idea of incarnation that I have made central to this study points to what is at issue in the twofold desire of theorists and theologians: the desire to engage in reflection and the desire to resist the charge that those reflections fail to engage the realities on which they reflect.

Bloom's conception of poetic experience (a distillation of essentially human experience) flows from what I have called a hyperspiritualist stance. As self-proclaimed gnostic, Bloom finds the body—indeed, nature in its broadest sense—to be the realm of a fatal necessity: a realm that would stifle any human spirit too weak to escape it. Embracing various spirit-body dualisms for the sake of separating spirit from body, Bloom's hyperspiritualist vision is profoundly anti-incarnational. Christian theologians will recognize that Bloom brings to human beings the Docetic view that heretical Christians once applied (and still apply) to the person of Christ (*Docetism* comes from the Greek *dokein*, meaning "to seem"). Docetists regarded Christ as a human being in appearance only; he only seemed to have a body, but he really was a fully divine (and therefore unembodied) being, the *logos*. In similar fashion, Bloom locates the real human being in the *pneuma* (spirit) or spark: he is concerned only with what he calls "the poet in the poet," by which he means the disembodied poetic imagination in the form of spirit, which resides (but is not essentially related to) the poet as embodied person. The grandeur of Bloom's embattled humanism is that the essential human being as spirit unceasingly battles against a threatened incarnation.

De Man's views are just as anti-incarnational as Bloom's, but in the opposite way. The opposite of the ancient Christian heresy of Docetism was known as Ebionitism. If the Docetic Christ remains an unembodied deity, an Ebionite Christ is never more than a human being. I have called de Man's reduction of all meaning (and ultimately, of all reality) to modes of textuality—modes of the intrinsic linguistic functioning of language as such—hypertextuality. Christian theologians will recognize that, if one imagines meaning as *logos* and text as human being, de Man's insistence that textuality reveals only the perpetual absence of meaning becomes an analogue to the Ebionite insistence that Christ is, has always been, and will always be merely human.

Putting together the cosmic reach of the classical Christian doctrine of incarnation with the comparable scope of the theoretical proposals offered by Bloom and de Man leads me to the following reflections. The Christian account of incarnation insists that ultimate meaning has become mysteriously but deeply integrated with all the material stuff of life, of the here and now. In contrast, Bloom insists that meaning is to be found elsewhere, while de Man insists that meaning is simply not to be found. Together, Bloom and de Man depict with unusual intensity and purity the twin poles of the incarnational imagination relieved of its paradoxical character. Christian theologians can benefit from reading the two theorists because the incarnational imagination requires one to take each pole with absolute seriousness. Indeed, it may be far better to grasp one of the poles firmly than to grasp neither while satisfying oneself that both have been grasped at once.

This latter possibility emerged when we turned from Bloom and de Man to Bakhtin. Christian theologians who read earlier versions of this book breathed sighs of relief upon arriving at chapter 3's discussion of Bakhtin. Here, at last, was a fellow traveler whose vision, however idiosyncratic and obscure, was yet recognizably Christian and whose key category of embodiment offered a satisfying interpretation of some of the complexities of the human situation. Some nontheological readers had nearly the opposite reaction: to them, the visions of Bloom and de Man, though admittedly severe or disenchanting, seemed recognizably and courageously in touch with actual human experience. In contrast, the synthesizing, holistic vision of Bakhtin seemed too distanced, too self-assured, overly serene.

My own view differs from both of these assessments. On the one hand, Bakhtin does seem to recognize something of the intensity of each of the twin poles: his discussion of the "unfinalized spirit" reflects the striving for originality central to Bloom's spirit; and his discussion of the way human beings fail to know all they wish to know echoes something of de Man's view of the continual absence of meaning and truth. On the other hand, Bakhtin locates these Bloomian and de Manian moments on a plane different from the aesthetic dimension in which consummation takes place. From Bakhtin's point of view, Bloom's and de Man's insights are appropriate to the ethical and epistemological realm of human life—the realm he calls inner body and spirit. But he argues that this realm by its very nature cannot provide the stance from which to discern human life in its wholeness, in its outer body and soul. Outer body and soul cannot be discerned or attained from within the ethical or epistemological realms; for this, we need the perspective of an other who can embody or consummate us by means of an outward perspective. Human beings, not as characters in a novel but as the enactors of their lives, require a supreme author or deity. And here we reach the point at which the nontheological reader (and the nontheologian in the theologian), persuaded by the more severe insights of Bloom and de Man, is likely to be put off. This seems to be the worst sort of evasion or deflection—a recuperation of holistic vision, a reconstitution of a fragmented vessel by papering over the cracks with an aestheticized theism.

I suggested in the introduction that, at the end of the day, theism would intrude into our discussion. Theism requires the sort of shift in planes that Bakhtin makes. Bakhtin inserts a God's-eye point of view, insisting that one cannot grasp the truth of human existence without it. What might make his insertion of the divine point of view more compelling than comparable moves by others is precisely the literary and phenomenological way in which he tries to characterize its inevitability. Bakhtin wants to paint a picture of literary authorship together with an account of humanity that makes particular embodiment central, in order to paint a picture that, in its fullest extent, will be implausible—indeed, unintelligible—without the ultimate authorship of human life by an Other.

It is not as though Bakhtin's theistic perspective simply flies in the face of the accounts of the human condition offered by Bloom and de Man. Rather, Bakhtin seems to say something like this: You can certainly hold views like those offered by Bloom and de Man, and you would not be wrong to do so. But you need to recognize the limits of those standpoints, for they will systematically, as a matter of their own principles, both posit and fail to attain meaning and significance for a human life. Granted, one can turn this liability into an asset: one can insist, with Albert Camus and Jean-Paul Sartre, that the very unattainability of meaning and significance has a meaning and significance all its own. But this, in Bakhtin's eyes, is to be heroic without ever becoming a hero (you can be heroic by risking your life for others, but only the regard of others can make you a hero). One of the merits of Bakhtin's account is that he does not suggest that views like those of Bloom and de Man are deficient as such, but only insofar as they claim a wider scope than they are entitled to: that is, only when such views become modes of theoreticism do they become not merely limited but false. Of course, we soon reach the point at which all charges can be turned back against Bakhtin: if Bloom's and de Man's visions overstep themselves by assuming their own nontheistic surrogates for a God's-eye point of view, cannot the same be said about Bakhtin's vision? Whether one accepts Bakhtin's claim that those other views are limited and need to be inserted into his more comprehensive view of things probably turns in the end on whether one thinks that otherness is both irreducible and productive. Such a view of the other is unavailable to both Bloom and de Man because their monisms of spirit and text ensure that neither one makes another person's point of view productive for his theories. For Bloom, the view of the other, in the form of a poem, is there to be misread by the ephebe. For de Man, there is no need of any other at all; we are all equally the pawns of language, and we will suffer our own private fates at its hands. Bakhtin's shift to the perspective of the other—the shift to the aesthetic plane where actual wholeness can be perceived for the first time—asserts that the way to address the limits of Bloom's frustrated quest for originality and de Man's acknowledgment of meaning's absence is to recognize that there is a vital dimension of human existence that is fundamentally not about originality and meaning, but about the loving acceptance by the other, apart from one's striving. Seen from the perspective of God as other and author of human existence, human life is not finally about the liberation of spirit from the grasp of the given (though it must include something of that quest), nor is it finally about the recognition that meaning sought is forever deferred (though it must include something of that insight). Rather, it is about the way all of those things (which, despite their status as genuinely human, in and by themselves never add up to anything complete or fully realized) do receive unification, integration, and wholeness—but only in the hands of another.

Even if one were willing to grant Bakhtin his move to another plane, on which the other provides the needed wholeness, one might still want to fault him for making such a move seem so easy and nonproblematic. It all seems so simple: regard one's life as though one were the hero of a novel authored by God; realize that one's striving remains unfulfilled and unfulfillable by oneself; accept the wholeness bequeathed by those around one—and ultimately by God. I agree that this vision, simply as a vision or second-order account, *is* easy—easy in the way that reading or watching a comedy in which others participate is easy, indeed often escapist. But Bakhtin's vision has its own kind of difficulty: the difficulty of living a life that looks and feels entirely like a tragedy while nonetheless continuing to trust that it is, in some more fundamentally enduring way, a comedy.

To regard Bakhtin's world as one in which all are busy fulfilling one another's lack and consummating one another, in which all are ultimately going to achieve fulfillment, is easy as long as one abstracts oneself from that vision. But it is not so easy, I think, to see oneself as standing in that world, to retain in all their severity Bloom's and de Man's insights that Bakhtin himself regards as inevitable and very real, and then, nevertheless, to go on trusting that one is living out a comedy rather than a tragedy. It is that "nevertheless" that pinpoints the site of the difficulty. That site is not in the realm of abstracted theory or theoreticism, but rather in the incarnate world: the world in which tragic struggle and stoic lack are brought together with comedic consummation, related but unmerged, distinguished but not separated, united hypostatically. And the hypostasis at issue here is not the divine Word but the human person.

All three literary theories, like the Christian theologies they partially compete with and overlap, gain whatever plausibility they have by taking their proponents back to the first-order realities of actual human existence. Bakhtin's vision suggests that the plausibility of theory and theology for life is tested only in life's enactment, which is to say, in nontheoretical and nontheological ways. That is where the truth of theory and theology will be tested. We regularly evade that test by setting up matching games, asking: Does this bit of performance or belief match some antecedentally existing description that we take to be normative (Scripture, doctrine, linguistics, science, psychoanalysis, and so on)? But all such matching games make sense only when the incarnational imagination has failed: only if I have first presupposed the divergence of meaning and existence will I be tempted to convince myself of the truth of a proposal about the meaning of existence by trying to match what I take to be existence as it really is with some presently appealing description of its meaning.

The incarnational imagination works the other way around. It presupposes that existence is already meaningful because the only relevant match has already been made—and here, match is just our own misleading way of putting the matter, our way of regarding a whole as a duality by forgetting that we were the ones who first decided to divide it. Christians long ago decided that perceiving the truth of that match comes, if at all, only eschatologically. Only from that perspective called "kingdom of heaven" could one gain a view of sufficient "otherness" to understand the truth of that match—to understand that this is the only possible correct match, to understand that this is what reality actually is, to understand that here is the point at which one can finally let things be—because that is what they are. From time to time, literary theorists express similar insights, as in Walter Benjamin's "pure language," de Man's "impossible combination" of symbol and allegory, or Bakhtin's insistence that theory be "rendered immanent" or "adequate" to life.

Bakhtin's literary account of the author/hero relation, as an extrapolation from a theological account of human life, is not an effort to evade the truths of unrealized eschatology, nor to indulge in premature proclamations of a fully realized eschatology. Rather, it is an effort to give an eschatologically informed description of things as they presently are, precisely because one cannot grasp the truth of things as they presently are apart from what they are destined to be. The stance of the consummating author is the literary or discursive reflection of the essential stance of Christian faith—the confidence that the most truthful accounts of reality are not the accounts that a reality uninformed by an eschatological vision gives of itself. But it has been the obverse side of that confidence that has provided the rationale for this book about literary theory directed at theologians: the recognition that visions of reality uninformed by that eschatological perspective offer insights that Christian theology ignores at the expense of its fullest and most nuanced account of reality's presently unconsummated character.

Abbreviations

AH Mikhail Bakhtin, "Author and Hero in Aesthetic Activity," in *Art and Answerability: Early Philosophical Essays by M. M. Bakhtin,* ed. Michael Holquist and Vadim Liapunov, trans. and notes by Vadim Liapunov, Supplement trans. Kenneth Brostrom, Univ. of Texas Press Slavic Series 9, ed. Michael Holquist (Austin: Univ. of Texas Press, 1990).

AI Harold Bloom, *The Anxiety of Influence: A Theory of Poetry* (New York: Oxford Univ. Press, 1973).

BM Harold Bloom, "'Before Moses Was, I Am': The Original and the Belated Testaments," in *The Bible,* Modern Critical Views, ed. Harold Bloom (New York: Chelsea House, 1987).

CS Martin Luther, *Confession Concerning Christ's Supper,* trans. and ed. Robert H. Fischer, *Luther's Works* 37 (Philadelphia: Fortress Press, 1961).

DN Mikhail Bakhtin, "Discourse in the Novel," in *The Dialogic Imagination: Four Essays by M. M. Bakhtin,* ed. Michael Holquist, trans. Caryl Emerson and Michael Holquist, Univ. of Texas Press Slavic Series 1 (Austin: Univ. of Texas Press, 1981).

MM Harold Bloom, *A Map of Misreading* (New York: Oxford Univ. Press, 1975).

OCD Augustine, *On Christian Doctrine,* trans. D. W. Robertson, Jr., The Library of Liberal Arts (Indianapolis: Bobbs-Merrill Educational Publishing, 1972).

PA   Mikhail Bakhtin, *Toward a Philosophy of the Act,* ed. Michael Holquist, trans. and notes by Vadim Liapunov (Austin: Univ. of Texas Press, 1993).

RP   Paul de Man, "Rhetoric of Persuasion (Nietzsche)," in *Allegories of Reading: Figural Language in Rousseau, Nietzsche, Rilke, and Proust* (New Haven: Yale Univ. Press, 1979).

RST   Harold Bloom, *Ruin the Sacred Truths: Poetry and Belief from the Bible to the Present* (Cambridge, Mass.: Harvard Univ. Press, 1989).

RT   Paul de Man, "The Rhetoric of Temporality," in *Blindness and Insight: Essays in the Rhetoric of Contemporary Criticism,* 2d ed., Theory and History of Literature 7 (Minneapolis: Univ. of Minnesota Press, 1983).

SD   Paul de Man, "Shelley Disfigured," in *The Rhetoric of Romanticism* (New York: Columbia Univ. Press, 1984).

ST   St. Thomas Aquinas, *Summa Theologiae.* Latin text and English translation, Introductions, Notes, Appendices, and Glossaries. Vol. 5: *God's Will and Providence* (Ia19–26), ed. and trans. Thomas Gilby, O.P. (Cambridge, England: Blackfriars, 1967).

TA   Roman Jakobson, "Two Aspects of Language and Two Types of Aphasic Disturbance," in *Fundamentals of Language,* 2d ed., ed. Roman Jakobson and Morris Halle (Paris: Mouton, 1975).

TB   Jacques Derrida, "The Tower of Babel," trans. Joseph F. Graham, in *Difference in Translation,* ed. Joseph F. Graham (Ithaca, N.Y.: Cornell Univ. Press, 1985).

WS   Harold Bloom, *Wallace Stevens: The Poems of Our Climate* (Ithaca, N.Y.: Cornell Univ. Press, 1977).

Notes

Introduction

1. For a recent theological criticism of postmodernist theory, see John Milbank, *Theology and Social Theory: Beyond Secular Reason* (Oxford, England: Blackwell, 1990). For a recent theoretical criticism of some literary manifestations of religious and theological notions, see Steven Cassedy, *Flight from Eden: The Origins of Modern Literary Criticism and Theory* (Berkeley and Los Angeles: Univ. of California Press, 1990), especially part 2 on the theological dimension of modern literary theory.

2. Ludwig Feuerbach, *The Essence of Christianity*, trans. George Eliot (New York: Harper & Row, 1957); Kenneth Burke, *The Rhetoric of Religion: Studies in Logology* (Berkeley: Univ. of California Press, 1970).

3. The term *classical Christian,* as well as similar terms such as *traditional* or *consensus,* are meant to suggest that the views described are broadly representative of the Christian tradition and would be acknowledged as such by most Christians. The terms are not meant to imply that such views have not been challenged, or that different or opposing views are not equally entitled to be regarded as Christian.

4. See Rudolf Bultmann, "New Testament and Mythology," in *Kerygma and Myth: A Theological Debate,* ed. Hans Werner Bartsch, trans. Reginald H. Fuller (New York: Harper & Row, 1953; rev. ed. Harper Torchbooks, 1961), 1–44.

5. See Hermann Samuel Reimarus, *Fragments,* ed. Charles H. Talbert, trans. Ralph S. Fraser (Philadelphia: Fortress Press, 1970); Frank Kermode, *The Genesis of Secrecy: On the Interpretation of Narrative* (Cambridge, Mass.: Harvard Univ. Press, 1979).

6. Harold Bloom, *The Anxiety of Influence: A Theory of Poetry* (New York: Oxford Univ. Press, 1973); Harold Bloom, *A Map of Misreading* (New York: Oxford Univ. Press, 1975); *Wallace Stevens: The Poems of Our Climate* (Ithaca, N.Y.: Cornell Univ. Press, 1977).

7. A point made by Jean-Pierre Mileur, *Literary Revisionism and the Burden of Modernity* (Berkeley: Univ. of California Press, 1985), 57, in Norman Finkelstein, *The Ritual of New Creation: Jewish Tradition and Contemporary Literature* (Albany: State Univ. of New York Press, 1992), 34.

8. Ferdinand de Saussure, *Course in General Linguistics*, ed. Charles Bally, Albert Sechehaye, and Albert Reidlinger, trans. Wade Baskin (New York: Philosophical Library, 1959).

9. Paul de Man, "The Rhetoric of Temporality," in *Blindness and Insight: Essays in the Rhetoric of Contemporary Criticism*, 2d ed., Theory and History of Literature, vol. 7 (Minneapolis: Univ. of Minnesota Press, 1983), 187–228; "Rhetoric of Persuasion (Nietzsche)," in *Allegories of Reading: Figural Language in Rousseau, Nietzsche, Rilke, and Proust* (New Haven: Yale Univ. Press, 1979), 119–131; "Shelley Disfigured," in *The Rhetoric of Romanticism* (New York: Columbia Univ. Press, 1984), 93–123. For a comprehensive and insightful study of de Man's work, see Christopher Norris, *Paul de Man: Deconstruction and the Critique of Aesthetic Ideology* (New York: Routledge, 1988).

10. A useful overview of de Man's career is provided by Lindsay Waters, "Paul de Man: Life and Works," in *Paul de Man: Critical Writings 1953–1978*, ed. Lindsay Waters, Theory and History of Literature, vol. 66 (Minneapolis: Univ. of Minnesota Press, 1989).

11. Mikhail Bakhtin, "Author and Hero in Aesthetic Activity," in *Art and Answerability: Early Philosophical Essays by M. M. Bakhtin*, ed. Michael Holquist and Vadim Liapunov, trans. and notes by Vadim Liapunov, Supplement trans. Kenneth Brostrom (Austin: Univ. of Texas Press, 1990); M. M. Bakhtin, *Toward a Philosophy of the Act*, trans. Michael Holquist, trans. and notes by Vadim Liapunov (Austin: Univ. of Texas Press, 1993).

12. Athanasius, *On the Incarnation of the Word* 45, trans. Archibald Robertson in *Christology of the Later Fathers*, The Library of Christian Classics, ed. Edward Rochie Hardy with Cyril C. Richardson (Philadelphia: Westminster Press, 1954), 100.

13. Augustine, *On Christian Doctrine*, trans. D. W. Robertson, Jr., The Library of Liberal Arts (Indianapolis: Bobbs-Merrill Educational Publishing, 1972), 1.12.12.

14. Karl Rahner, *Foundations of the Christian Faith: An Introduction to the Idea of Christianity*, trans. William V. Dych (New York: Crossroad, 1982), 87.

15. On the place of apologetics in Christian reflection, see William Werpehowski, "Ad Hoc Apologetics," *Journal of Religion* 66 (1986), 282–301; William C. Placher, *Unapologetic Theology: A Christian Voice in a Pluralistic Conversation* (Louisville, Ky.: Westminster/John Knox Press, 1989).

16. Karl Barth, "The Humanity of God," in *Karl Barth: Theologian of Freedom*, ed. Clifford Green, The Making of Modern Theology (Minneapolis: Fortress Press, 1991), 58–59.

17. Karl Barth, "*Fiat Iustitia*," in *Karl Barth*, 259.

18. See Hans W. Frei, "Ad Hoc Correlation," in *Types of Christian Theology*, ed. George Hunsinger and William C. Placher (New Haven: Yale Univ. Press, 1992), 70–91.

1.   Spirit and Revision

1. Roman Jakobson, "Two Aspects of Language and Two Types of Aphasic Disturbance," in *Fundamentals of Language*, 2d ed., ed. Roman Jakobson and Morris Halle (Paris: Mouton, 1975), 69–96, hereafter TA.

2. James Preus, *From Shadow to Promise: Old Testament Interpretation from Augustine to the Young Luther* (Cambridge, Mass.: Harvard Univ. Press, Belknap Press, 1969).

3. TA, 93.
4. TA, 75–76.
5. See Herbert Marks, "Pauline Typology and Revisionary Criticism," in *The Bible*, Modern Critical Views, ed. Harold Bloom (New York: Chelsea House, 1987), 305–21.
6. Here de Man follows Friedrich Nietzsche who, in part 2 of *On the Genealogy of Morals*, trans. Walter Kaufmann and R. J. Hollingdale (New York: Random House, 1967), undermines notions of a self sufficiently self-continuous to be able to hold itself accountable for its earlier actions. This theoretical position is full of implications when placed next to de Man's silence (reported by his closest colleagues) regarding his own early biography.
7. Paul de Man, "Rhetoric of Persuasion (Nietzsche)," in *Allegories of Reading: Figural Language in Rousseau, Nietzsche, Rilke, and Proust* (New Haven: Yale Univ. Press, 1989), 129; hereafter RP.
8. RP, 125.
9. Ibid. Bracketed inserts and emphasis are de Man's; parenthetical inserts are Nietzsche's.
10. Ibid.
11. Augustine, *On Christian Doctrine*, trans. D. W. Robertson, Jr., The Library of Liberal Arts (Indianapolis: Bobbs-Merrill Educational Publishing, 1972), 3.5.9; hereafter *OCD*.
12. *OCD* 3.6.10.
13. *OCD* 3.8.12.
14. *OCD* 3.9.13.
15. Ibid.
16. Ibid.
17. In this text, Augustine's use of the terms *Israelite* and *Jew* is hermeneutical rather than strictly historical. Rather than drawing a historical distinction between First Temple and post-Second Temple Judaism, Augustine is distinguishing two different ways of reading Scripture.
18. RP, 123.
19. RP, 125.
20. RP, 123.
21. RP, 127.
22. RP, 129.
23. RP, 131.
24. *OCD* 3.6.10.
25. RP, 127.
26. RP, 129.
27. RP, 127.
28. Harold Bloom, *Kabbala and Criticism* (New York: Continuum, 1975), 86.
29. In part 2 of *A Map of Misreading* (New York: Oxford Univ. Press, 1975), hereafter *MM*, Bloom describes the key terms of his system (the "map") and illustrates them through a close reading of Robert Browning's "Childe Roland." For a comprehensive, general introduction to Bloom, see David Fite, *Harold Bloom: The Rhetoric of Romantic Vision* (Amherst: Univ. of Massachusetts Press, 1985). For a somewhat more complex treatment of Bloom in relation to modern literary theory, see Jean-Pierre Mileur, *Literary Revisionism and the Burden of Modernity* (Berkeley: Univ. of California Press, 1985).
30. Wallace Stevens, "Domination of Black," in *The Palm at the End of the Mind:*

Selected Poems and a Play by Wallace Stevens, ed. Holly Stevens (New York: Vintage Books, 1972), 14–15.

31. Percy Bysshe Shelley, "Ode to the West Wind," in *English Romantic Writers,* ed. David Perkins (New York: Harcourt Brace Jovanovich, 1967), 1026–27, lines 1–14.

32. Paul de Man, "Review of Bloom's *Anxiety of Influence,*" Appendix A in *Blindness and Insight: Essays in the Rhetoric of Contemporary Criticism,* 2d ed., Theory and History of Literature, vol. 7 (Minneapolis: Univ. of Minnesota Press, 1983), 267–76.

33. Harold Bloom, *Wallace Stevens: The Poems of Our Climate* (Ithaca, N.Y.: Cornell Univ. Press, 1977), 386; hereafter *WS.*

34. *WS,* 392.

35. *WS,* 393.

36. Ibid.

37. *WS,* 392–93.

38. *WS,* 393.

39. *WS,* 393, 394–95.

40. *MM,* 48.

41. Harold Bloom, *The Anxiety of Influence: A Theory of Poetry* (New York: Oxford Univ. Press, 1973), 20–21; hereafter *AI.*

42. See *"Daemonization* or the Counter-Sublime," chapter 4 in *AI,* 99–112.

43. *AI,* 20.

44. Harold Bloom, *Blake's Apocalypse: A Study in Poetic Argument* (1963; reprint, Ithaca, N.Y.: Cornell Univ. Press, 1970), 348, as quoted in Fite, 58.

45. *MM,* 116.

46. The following exposition of Luther's changing interpretation of the Psalms is based on Preus's discussion in *From Shadow to Promise,* 166–75.

47. Martin Luther, "Psalm Fifty-One," in *First Lectures on the Psalms I, Psalms 1–75,* trans. Herbert J. A. Bouman, ed. H. C. Oswald, *Luther's Works* 10 (St. Louis: Concordia, 1974), 240.

48. Harold Bloom, *Ruin the Sacred Truths: Poetry and Belief from the Bible to the Present* (Cambridge, Mass.: Harvard Univ. Press, 1989), 43; hereafter *RST.*

49. *AI,* 92.

50. Fite, *Harold Bloom,* 26.

51. *MM,* 75.

52. Sacvan Bercovitch, *The Puritan Origins of the American Self* (New Haven and London: Yale Univ. Press, 1975), 163–74.

53. *AI,* 43.

54. Harold Bloom, "'Before Moses Was, I Am': The Original and the Belated Testaments," in *The Bible,* Modern Critical Views, ed. Harold Bloom (New York: Chelsea House, 1987), 291, 292; hereafter *BM.*

55. *BM,* 297.

56. *BM,* 298.

57. See Marks, "Pauline Typology."

58. *RST,* 43.

59. *MM,* 96.

60. *MM,* 76.

61. *WS,* 386–87.

62. *RST,* 112.

63. *WS,* 387.

64. *RST,* 131.

65. *WS,* 393.

66. *WS,* 396.

67. Ibid. Bloom is quoting from an unidentified work by John Hollander.

68. When Bloom is not making a point about Christianity's failed struggle with the Hebrew Bible, he tends to view both classical Judaism and classical Christianity as parts of one "normative tradition, Jewish or Christian" *(RST,* 18). So assimilation at certain points would not be surprising.

69. Martin Luther, *First Lectures on the Psalms II, Psalms 76–126,* trans. Herbert J. A. Bouman, ed. Hilton C. Oswald, *Luther's Works* 11 (St. Louis: Concordia, 1976), 298.

70. Ibid., 305.

71. Ibid., 298–99.

72. Ibid., 299.

73. Ibid.

74. *RST,* 135.

2. Text and Performance

1. Paul de Man, "Allegory *(Julie),"* in *Allegories of Reading: Figural Language in Rousseau, Nietzsche, Rilke, and Proust* (New Haven: Yale Univ. Press, 1979), 218–19.

2. Ibid., 218, 219.

3. Martin Luther, *Confession Concerning Christ's Supper,* in *Word and Sacrament III,* ed. and trans. Robert H. Fischer, *Luther's Works* 37 (Philadelphia: Fortress Press, 1961); hereafter *CS.*

4. Note that this is not the same as saying that the humanity is the divinity, or vice versa. Luther's entire point will be lost unless one grants the possibility of a unity of natures in a person that does not require the equivalence of natures.

5. *CS,* 206.

6. *CS,* 210.

7. *CS,* 211.

8. *CS,* 212–13.

9. *CS,* 183.

10. *CS,* 184.

11. *CS,* 188.

12. *CS,* 207–8.

13. *CS,* 193.

14. *CS,* 191.

15. Paul de Man, "The Rhetoric of Temporality," in *Blindness and Insight: Essays in the Rhetoric of Contemporary Criticism,* 2d ed., Theory and History of Literature, vol. 7 (Minneapolis: Univ. of Minnesota Press, 1983), 206–7; hereafter RT.

16. Walter Benjamin, "The Task of the Translator," in *Illuminations,* trans. Harry Zohn, ed. Hannah Arendt (New York: Schocken, 1969), 69–82. For the German text, see Benjamin, "Die Aufgabe des Übersetzers," in *Gesammelte Schriften* IV.1, ed. Tillman Rexroth, Werkausgabe Band 10 (Frankfurt: Suhrkamp, 1972), 9–21.

17. Paul de Man, "Conclusions: Walter Benjamin's The Task of the Translator," in *The Resistance to Theory* (Minneapolis: Univ. of Minnesota Press, 1986).

18. Benjamin, "Task of the Translator," 78, emphasis added.

19. Carol Jacobs, "The Monstrosity of Translation," *Modern Language Notes* 90 (1975), 755–66.

20. Jacobs, 762, including bracketed material; emphasis added. Benjamin wrote *Bruchstück*, which Jacobs translates accurately as a singular "broken part." De Man, despite appealing to Jacob's translation, uses the plural "broken parts," a difference that serves to support his reading of the passage. It is important to remember, however, that de Man's essay is actually a written transcription by others of a recording of remarks de Man delivered orally.

21. De Man, "Conclusions," 90.

22. Ibid., 91.

23. Jacques Derrida, "The Tower of Babel," trans. Joseph F. Graham, in *Difference in Translation*, ed. Joseph F. Graham (Ithaca, N.Y. and London: Cornell Univ. Press, 1985), 165–207; hereafter TB. For Derrida's French text, see "Des Tours de Babel," pp. 209–48 in the same volume.

24. TB, 187.

25. TB, 186–87.

26. TB, 188.

27. TB, 186–87.

28. TB, 191.

29. *CS*, 223.

30. *CS*, 226–27.

31. *CS*, 229.

32. *CS*, 219ff.

33. *CS*, 230.

34. *CS*, 221.

35. *CS*, 222.

36. *CS*, 221.

37. *CS*, 222.

38. Martin Luther, *Lectures on Galatians 1535, Chapters 1–4*, trans. Jaroslav Pelikan, *Luther's Works* 26 (St. Louis: Concordia, 1963), 129–30.

39. See David Dawson, "Against the Divine Ventriloquist: Coleridge and De Man on Symbol, Allegory, and Scripture," *Literature and Theology*, 4:3 (November 1990), 293–310.

40. See "Paradox" in the glossary for the distinction between conceptual and Christian paradox.

41. See John Milbank, "Signs Without Substance: Christianity, Signs, Origins," in *Literature and Theology*, part 1, 2:1 (March 1988), 1–17; part 2, 2:2 (September 1988), 133–52.

42. Paul de Man, "Shelley Disfigured," in *The Rhetoric of Romanticism* (New York: Columbia Univ. Press, 1984), 95; hereafter SD.

43. SD, 94, 121.

44. SD, 120. De Man's move in this sentence from the specific "fracture" of Shelley's text to the general, universalizing claim that the same fracture "lies hidden in *all* texts" (emphasis added) marks the point at which his reading of Shelley's poem becomes explicitly "theoretical"—an expression of his own general theory of the way all language engages in self-deconstruction. I will leave to other, more informed readers an assessment of the extent to which this move from first-order literary criticism to second-order literary theory might betray de Man's otherwise moral act of attempting, by means of his critical essay, to relate to the unique text, body, and person of the dead Shelley.

45. SD, 121.

46. SD, 123.

47. SD, 121.
48. SD, 123.
49. SD, 122.
50. SD, 100.
51. P. B. Shelley, *The Triumph of Life*, in *English Romantic Writers*, ed. David Perkins (New York: Harcourt Brace Jovanovich, 1967), 1061–68. I have inserted brackets to indicate where the editor has identified lacunae in the poem.
52. SD, 112.
53. Ibid.
54. *Triumph*, ll. 339–42; 375–77, emphasis added.
55. SD, 113.
56. Ibid.
57. Ibid.
58. SD, 114.
59. Ibid.
60. Ibid.
61. SD, 115.
62. Ibid.
63. SD, 116.
64. Christian theologians need to resist de Man's easy equation of "natural" and "mediated": the triune deity is mediated but not natural. Likewise, they must resist the equation of singularity and violence: the triune deity is one, but essentially peaceful; the Spirit is *vinculum pacis inter Patrem et Filium* (bond of peace between the Father and the Son)—Karl Barth, "Concluding Unscientific Postscript on Schleiermacher," in *Karl Barth: Theologian of Freedom*, ed. Clifford Green (Minneapolis: Fortress Press, 1991), 88.
65. SD, 117.
66. Ibid.
67. SD, 116.
68. SD, 116–17.
69. SD, 117.
70. Ibid.
71. SD, 118. Shelley's deeply painful awareness in this poem of the inevitability of such a falsifying and inauthentic recuperative tendency lends support to those who argue that his death was not an accident but a suicide, a recognition that the visionary quest of Romantic poetics, as well as his own personal life, had ended in failure.
72. SD, 117–18.
73. SD, 118.
74. SD, 118–19.
75. SD, 119.
76. Ibid.
77. Ibid.
78. SD, 120.
79. See Minae Mizumura, "Renunciation," in *The Lesson of Paul de Man*, Yale French Studies no. 69, ed. Peter Brooks, Shoshana Felman, and J. Hillis Miller (New Haven: Yale Univ. Press, 1985), 81–97.
80. Paul de Man, "The Dead-End of Formalist Criticism," in *Blindness and Insight*, 245.
81. Gnosticism is generally thought of as a dualistic worldview, but, at least in

the Valentinian form that Bloom admires, is more accurately understood as a protest against dualism in the name of monism. See David Dawson, *Allegorical Reading and Cultural Revision in Ancient Alexandria* (Berkeley and Los Angeles: Univ. of California Press, 1992), chapter 3 ("Valentinus: The Apocalypse of the Mind") and pp. 283–84, n. 45.

82. Harold Bloom, *The Anxiety of Influence: A Theory of Poetry* (New York: Oxford Univ. Press, 1973), 85–86.

83. Harold Bloom, *The American Religion: The Emergence of the Post-Christian Nation* (New York: Simon & Schuster, 1992), 58, 114.

84. John Milton, *Paradise Lost,* in *Complete Poems and Major Prose,* ed. Merritt Y. Hughes (Indianapolis: Odyssey, 1957), 211–469.

85. John Milbank, *Theology and Social Theory: Beyond Secular Reason* (Oxford: Blackwell, 1990), 289.

86. Harold Bloom, *A Map of Misreading* (New York: Oxford Univ. Press, 1975), 10.

87. Milbank, *Theology and Social Theory,* 289.

88. Harold Bloom, *Wallace Stevens: The Poems of Our Climate* (Ithaca, N.Y.: Cornell Univ. Press, 1977), 388.

89. Ibid., 387.

90. Friedrich Nietzsche, *On the Genealogy of Morals,* trans. Walter Kaufmann and R. J. Hollingdale (New York: Random House, 1967), First Essay, section 10, p. 39.

91. Mizumura, "Renunciation," 97.

3. Body and Consummation

1. See Caryl Emerson, "Russian Orthodoxy and the Early Bakhtin," *Religion & Literature* 22.2–3 (Summer-Autumn 1990), 109–131.

2. Mikhail Bakhtin, "Author and Hero in Aesthetic Activity," in *Art and Answerability: Early Philosophical Essays by M. M. Bakhtin,* ed. Michael Holquist and Vadim Liapunov, trans. and notes by Vadim Liapunov, Supplement trans. Kenneth Brostrom, Univ. of Texas Press Slavic Series 9, ed. Michael Holquist (Austin: Univ. of Texas Press, 1990), hereafter AH; M. M. Bakhtin, *Toward a Philosophy of the Act,* ed. Michael Holquist, trans. and notes by Vadim Liapunov (Austin: Univ. of Texas Press, 1993), hereafter *PA;* M. M. Bakhtin, "Discourse in the Novel," in *The Dialogic Imagination: Four Essays by M. M. Bakhtin,* ed. Michael Holquist; trans. Caryl Emerson and Michael Holquist, Univ. of Texas Press Slavic Series 1 (Austin: Univ. of Texas Press, 1981), 259–422, hereafter DN. For a thorough and judicious introduction to Bakhtin's writings and ideas in the context of the evolution of his career, see Gary Saul Morson and Caryl Emerson, *Mikhail Bakhtin: Creation of a Prosaics* (Stanford, Calif.: Stanford Univ. Press, 1990).

3. See Katerina Clark and Michael Holquist, *Mikhail Bakhtin* (Cambridge, Mass.: Harvard Univ. Press, 1984), ix. Holquist argues elsewhere that Bakhtin sought to "completely rethink West European metaphysics in the light of religious thought," and that Orthodox theology was the wellspring of Bakhtin's work in the 1920s ("The Politics of Representation," in *Allegory and Representation: Selected Papers from the English Institute, 1979–80* [New Series, no. 5], ed. Stephen J. Greenblatt [Baltimore: Johns Hopkins Univ. Press, 1981], 171).

4. St. Thomas Aquinas, *Summa Theologiae* Ia22.2.ad.4 from vol. 5: *God's Will and Providence* (Ia19–26), ed. and trans. Thomas Gilby O.P. (Cambridge, England: Blackfriars, 1967); hereafter *ST.*

5. *ST* Ia22.3.
6. *ST* Ia23.5.
7. Karl Rahner, *Foundations of the Christian Faith: An Introduction to the Idea of Christianity*, trans. William V. Dych (New York: Crossroad, 1982), 79.
8. Ibid.
9. Ibid., 84.
10. AH, 82–83.
11. Ibid., 83.
12. Ibid.
13. AH, 114, emphasis added.
14. AH, 115, emphasis added.
15. Ibid.
16. AH, 116.
17. Ibid., emphasis added.
18. See Emerson, "Russian Orthodoxy," 115–16.
19. AH, 117–18.
20. *ST* Ia22.1.
21. AH, 118.
22. AH, 119.
23. Ibid.
24. AH, 90.
25. See AH, 84.
26. AH, 90.
27. AH, 92.
28. AH, 119.
29. *ST* Ia22.1.
30. AH, 18–19, emphasis added in second paragraph.
31. AH, 120.
32. Ibid.
33. AH, 56.
34. AH, 5.
35. AH, 25.
36. AH, 26.
37. AH, 78.
38. AH, 79.
39. Ibid.
40. Ibid.
41. AH, 131.
42. AH, 22.
43. Ibid.
44. AH, 8.
45. AH, 88.
46. DN, 327–28.
47. DN, 328.
48. Ibid.
49. Ibid.
50. Ibid.
51. See *PA,* 65–75.
52. DN, 278.
53. DN, 279.

54. DN, 331.
55. DN, 278.
56. DN, 405.
57. DN, 400.
58. Augustine, *On Christian Doctrine,* trans. D. W. Robertson, Jr., The Library of Liberal Arts (Indianapolis: Bobbs-Merrill Educational Publishing, 1972), 2.4.5–2.5.6.
59. DN, 331.
60. AH, 14.
61. AH, 84.
62. Ibid.
63. Ibid.
64. AH, 90.
65. AH, 106–7.
66. Paul de Man, "Shelley Disfigured," in *The Rhetoric of Romanticism* (New York: Columbia Univ. Press, 1984), 121.
67. Ibid., 122.
68. AH, 108.
69. Ibid.
70. AH, 123–24.
71. AH, 131.
72. *PA,* 64.
73. *PA,* 2.
74. Ibid.
75. *PA,* 21.
76. *PA,* 2.
77. *PA,* 55.
78. *PA,* 7.
79. *PA,* 9.
80. *PA,* 2–3.
81. *PA,* 18.
82. Ibid.
83. Ibid.
84. *PA,* 20.
85. *PA,* 18.
86. *PA,* 7.
87. *PA,* 61.
88. *PA,* 61–62.
89. Ibid. 62.
90. *PA,* 63–64.

Glossary

Aesthetization is Bakhtin's term for the process by which "the other" (person) "justifies," or "consummates," a subject's life, rendering it an accomplished, satisfying whole by providing something *transgredient* to the subject, that is, a perspective that the subject cannot provide for himself or herself (see also Consummation; Justification). This process is also called *aesthetic seeing* or *aesthetic love*. De Man's use of the term *aesthetic* differs from Bakhtin's. De Man uses the term to characterize a Romantic view of an essential relation of meaning to poetic image that he regards as self-mystifying and false (see also symbol under Deconstruction; recuperation under Troping).

Consummation has both literary and theological meanings. Bakhtin uses the term to refer to the completion of life provided by aesthetization (see also Aesthetization; Justification). Left to its own devices, human life remains free but *unfinalized,* failing to attain the knowledge or goodness it seeks. Consummation or *finalization* can only be provided by the perspective of another person, whose aestheticizing perspective grants to the other person his or her complete *embodiment*. In Christian theology, consummation refers to the final divine act of the three-act drama of reality or *economy of salvation* (creation, incarnation, consummation). The act of consummation involves the *second coming* or return of Christ to earth and the institution of the *kingdom of heaven* (or kingdom of God), a state in which the divine intention is fully realized. Reflections on consummation are *eschatological* reflections (from the Greek *eschatos,* "last"). Those who think that the kingdom of heaven is or will be realized on earth prior to the final consummation are proponents of *realized eschatology.* In the Eastern Christian tradition out of which Bakhtin emerges, the consummation of creation entails a transformation of human beings (their *divinization*) in which they become "like God" or "divine": "God became human so that human beings might become divine"—Athanasius (see also image of God under Trinity). Western interpretations of this event sometimes refer to the believer's *beatific vision* or direct encounter with God.

Conversion is a person's radical change or turn from one life orientation to another, including the change from no religion to a religion, from one religion to another, or from an ordinary to an extraordinary mode of religious life. Turning or converting from Judaism to Christianity generally entailed a rereading of the Hebrew Bible that discerned in the biblical narratives prefigurations (*figures* or *types*) of Christian truths (figural reading or *typology*) (see also Tropes; Troping). This form of reading turned the *Hebrew Bible* (the Scripture of Judaism) into a Christian *Old Testament* that found its prefigured fulfillment in the Christian *New Testament:* both testaments together comprise the *Christian Bible.* Christian efforts to reject the Old Testament as part of the Christian Bible, such as the second-century C.E. *Marcionite* movement, were deemed heretical.

Deconstruction is a literary theoretical application of a poststructuralist account of language to the understanding of the nature and functioning of literature (see also Structuralism); Jacques Derrida's deconstructive view of language emphasizes the way signifiers both differ from one another and actually defer the meaning they only seem to make present. De Man's view of deconstruction focuses on the *aporia* or constant *undecidability* (or *oscillation*) between *language as constative* (language that asserts that something is the case) and *language as performative* (language that, as a *speech act,* accomplishes, or posits, a new state of affairs). He links these two functions to two kinds of *rhetoric:* rhetoric as a set of tropes or figures of speech and rhetoric as oratory or persuasion. De Man calls the oscillation of language its *textuality* or *rhetoricity.* He also discovers the deconstructive function of language at work in the contrast between a literary *symbol* and an *allegory:* a symbol offers a meaning that falsely claims to be essentially or intrinsically connected to an image, while allegory accurately reveals the wholly artificial connection between meaning and image. De Man argues that symbols are forms of *synecdoche,* because symbolic meaning is intrinsically connected with the image as a part is essentially related to a whole (see also Tropes).

Dualism construes reality as consisting of two fundamentally different principles or entities. For example, the ancient religion of Manichaeism split reality into two utterly different and opposing forces (a good God of light and an evil God of darkness). The *disjunctive pattern* in Christian theological reflection, by stressing the difference between God and the world or between different forms of human experience verges toward a dualistic perspective. Bakhtin's *dialogism*—his insistence that reality consists of different voices or perspectives in their interchange and mutual interaction—is an effort to resist both monism and dualism while still being able to talk about the genuine unity and multiplicity of existence. His dialogism may therefore be contrasted with appeals to *mediating concepts* that would blur difference for the sake of achieving unity, and it might be compared with the methodological approach of this book—*ad hoc correlation*—that seeks to preserve differences while recognizing genuine commonality (see also Monism; Paradox).

Eucharist or "thanksgiving" is the word for the central Christian sacrament (also called *Lord's Supper* or Communion), a sacred meal of bread and wine in which Christ is present to believers. Views of the nature or manner of Christ's presence range from some form of *real presence* to various forms of symbolic or remembered presence. The efficacy of the sacrament in making Christ present is linked to the *words of institution* ("This is my body, this is my blood"), originally spoken by Jesus at the Last Supper and reinvoked in subsequent eucharistic celebrations. When literary theorists or others speak of the *sacramental presence* or *incarnational presence* of meaning in texts, they are highlighting (and generally criticizing) a view of language as analogous to the sacrament of the Eucharist: just as the Eucharist makes Christ present, so language (often symbolic language) is said to make meaning present (see also symbol under Deconstruction; de Man's use of *aesthetic* under Aesthetization).

Hermeneutics is the theory and method of interpretation (from *Hermēs*, messenger for the Greek gods). *Interpretation* is the process by which one discerns the meaning of a particular use of language. Hermeneutics may be as broad as an all-encompassing theory about human meaning and understanding (a *general hermeneutics*), or as narrow as a collection of particular techniques for reading certain kinds of texts (for example, legal hermeneutics, biblical hermeneutics). *Hermeneutical views of interpretation* distinguish between meaning and its representation in language, and are opposed by deconstructionists, who regard language as a textuality or rhetoricity that cannot be interpreted because it generates no meaning but only the undecidability of meaning (see Deconstruction). Bloom also opposes hermeneutical views of interpretation under what he calls *idealizing readings* that replace the struggle between authors with appeals to underlying continuities. Those who accept the hermeneutical view of interpretation, but remain skeptical that the apparent meaning is actually the real meaning, may engage in the *hermeneutics of suspicion:* for example, Freud argued that although dreams were meaningful and could be interpreted, their real meanings lay concealed beneath a series of misleading surface meanings.

Hypostatic union is the result of the self-*incarnation* or becoming "enfleshed" as the human being *Jesus of Nazareth* by the person of God the Son (or *logos*). The ancient *Creed of Chalcedon* (451 C.E.) describes the incarnate *logos* as "one person" (*hypostasis*) "in two natures" (*en duo physesin*), human and divine. *Naive incarnationalism* is a complaint by Chalcedonian Christians about what they would regard as a simplistic (and hence misleading) view of the hypostatic union as either an essentially unitive (Monophysite) or essentially disjunctive (Nestorian) combination of divine and human natures (see also Dualism; Monism). In their view, the Chalcedonian Creed specifically rules out unitive and disjunctive construals, insisting instead that the distinction of natures does not undermine the unity of the person, and that the unity of person does not blur the distinction of natures. Because of the unity of person, the attributes of both natures may be properly regarded as attributes of the same person—there is a mysterious "sharing of attributes" (*communicatio idiomatum*) via their union in a single person that allows the Christian to say, for example, that the Son of God died on the cross although the divine nature as such remained impassible, or that the Son of God bore the sins of humanity while not himself being sinful. Reflection on Jesus of Nazareth as God incarnate is known as *Christology.* One kind of christological reflection focuses on the self-emptying or *kenōsis* (Greek for "emptying") of God in the incarnation. Such *kenotic Christology* emphasizes the way in which God in the person of the Son seemingly gives up deity in order to become embodied as a human being (though the formulation remains paradoxical, contending that such giving up was in fact the fullest possible expression of divine power).

Justification in Christian theology refers to the act of God in Christ that brings the sinner back into proper relationship with God. In justifying the sinner, God either makes the sinner righteous by transforming him or her, or chooses, in view of Christ's sacrifice, to regard the sinner as righteous. The first option, advanced by Augustine and predominant in Roman Catholicism, stresses that "faith is formed by love" (*fides formata caritate*). The form of Protestant Christianity known as *Lutheranism* takes the second view, according to which the sinner who is regarded by God as righteous nevertheless remains a sinner: the justified Christian is *simul iustus et peccator* ("at once both a righteous person and a sinner"). As interpreted by the apostle Paul (and embraced by Christianity generally), the divine act of justification, like all divine acts, is unmerited by human beings, and the righteousness granted or attributed is wholly gratuitous, an act of divine *grace*. Bakhtin's use of justification to refer to the way a literary character's or a real person's life is fulfilled by the vision of an author or another person apart from the categories of meaning or purpose is analogous to this idea of divine grace (see also aesthetic love under Aesthetization).

Monism is a view of reality as consisting fundamentally of only one thing; differences within a monistic system are only superficial or apparent. Bakhtin protests against monistic views, which he calls *monological*—consisting of only a single voice or perspective and excluding competing, or simply different, points of view. He also protests against efforts to synthesize such differences in order to produce a *merger*. Critics of the *unitive pattern* in Christian theological reflection argue that such a perspective, by stressing the similarity of God and the world (as in G. W. F. Hegel's idealist philosophy) or the communality of experience (as in Friedrich Schleiermacher's hermeneutics), verges toward a monistic perspective (see also Dualism; Paradox).

Paradox is the radical superimposition of apparent irreconcilables. Chalcedonian Christian theology rejects both monism and dualism in favor of various paradoxical formulations that discern genuine unity amid apparent dualism while not obliterating difference. One can distinguish a conceptual paradox from paradoxes peculiar to Christianity, however. A *conceptual paradox* is the result of a logical contradiction (for example, the eternal is the temporal, the temporal is the eternal). *Paradoxes in Christianity* are believed to result from specific divine acts in space and time (for example, God becomes a human being; divine providence coexists with genuinely free human acts; the justified person remains a sinner). Such paradoxes may strike observers as combinations of logical incompatibles, but from a Christian point of view, the perception of logical impossibility does not limit what is possible but reflects the limitations of human knowledge, whether due to finitude, sin, or both. At the consummation, the fundamental rationality and intelligibility of divine acts that earlier appeared to be logically impossible may be revealed.

Representation takes place when language is used to stand for some nonlinguistic reality, or when one instance of language is used to stand for another. Representation is *epistemological* (from *epistēmē* or "knowledge") when language purports to offer a description of nonlinguistic reality. In this case, the description may consist of *concepts* (ideas, meanings) in the knower's mind. When the description matches reality accurately, we say that the description is not only meaningful but true; *truth* can be defined as the accurate match between a description and what is described.

Structuralism in linguistics analyzes language as a timeless structure or set of linguistic possibilities (*langue*) rather than as it is used in specific *speech acts* (*parole*). At least since the ancient Stoics, language has often been regarded as a system of signs: a *sign* consists of a verbal utterance or written mark (the *signifier*) and the meaning or concept associated with that utterance or mark (the *signified*); the object in the world to which the language user refers by means of the sign is called the *referent*. Christian theologians such as Luther and Augustine draw on sign theory in various ways. Structural linguists are interested in neither the referents of signs nor in their signified meanings as such, but only in the way such meanings are generated by the relations of the signifiers to one another, especially their differences from one another. *Poststructuralism* in literary theory takes structuralist insights one step further, contending that the differences between signifiers escape the constraints of all systems or structures and are both uncontrollable and infinite—a situation often called the *free play of the signifier* (see also Deconstruction).

Theology ranges from a speculative or metaphysical inquiry into the nature of God (and related matters such as world, human being, language, evil, and so on), to nonspeculative, self-descriptive accounts by specific, historical religious communities of their faith and practice. A religion itself in its direct performance of worship, prayer, and ethical behavior is said to produce *first-order discourse* (liturgies, prayers, moral actions). When religious persons stand back from, think about, and evaluate their first-order performance, they engage in a second-order reflection that produces *second-order discourse* (theological utterances and writings). When that discourse concerns theology's own procedures, theologians move toward the third-order or metareflection known as *theological method*.

Theoreticism is Bakhtin's term for the pernicious separation of theory from life—for the tendency of certain kinds of reflection (natural science and philosophy, historiography, and aesthetics) to become divorced from the actual experiences they seek to interpret. Bakhtin's protest against theoreticism can be understood as a rejection of any second-order discourse that fails to engage the very first-order performance that justifies its existence (see first-order discourse and second-order discourse under Theology). Theoreticism, aesthetic ideology, and *idealizing interpretations,* the respective targets of Bakhtin, de Man, and Bloom, all tend to obliterate particularity for the sake of homogenizing, global categories of reflection (see de Man's use of aesthetic under Aesthetization; idealizing readings under Hermeneutics).

Theory consists of a unified, comprehensive, conceptual construal of some subject matter. In the natural and social sciences, theory draws on various natural laws, sociological patterns, and experimental results in order to predict the behavior of as-yet-undiscovered phenomena or of old phenomena under novel circumstances. In the humanities, theory does not appeal to laws or make predictions; instead, theory (in the form of literary theory or theology) organizes diverse phenomena into large interpretative wholes that can be understood under broad categories. The humanities have recently taken a pragmatist turn that frowns on such theorizing because of its tendency to allow a few categories to dominate in ways that override important particularities and differences in order to serve special, hidden interests. Hence, much contemporary literary theory presents itself as *nontheoretical* or pragmatist; those who defend the importance of theoretical reflection often do so by construing it precisely as a mode of reflection that exposes the pitfalls of what currently goes under the rubric of "theory." Likewise, much contemporary Christian theological writing also opposes global theoretical categories in favor of theological reflection more directly rooted in, and circumscribed by, the particular language and practices of Christian communities.

Trinity describes the character of the Christian God as consisting of one divine *ousia* or "substance" and three *hypostases* or "persons" (Father, Son, and Holy Spirit). "Person" translates the Latin *persona*, which in turn translates the Greek *hypostasis;* the meaning of *hypostasis* (or *persona*) must be derived from its usage in trinitarian formulations and should not be confused with modern concepts of "person." The heart of the doctrine of the Trinity was defined by the Creed of Nicea in 325 C.E., though it was subject to much subsequent debate, elaboration, and refinement. The doctrine in its basic form declares that God consists of the person of the *Father*, who eternally begets the person of the *Son* (*Word* or *logos*). The Father and Son share the divine nature, but differ in that the Father is the uncreated and unbegotten begettor of the Son while the Son is begotten of the Father. From the relation between the Father and the Son (or, in Eastern Christianity, from the Father alone) proceeds a third person, the *Holy Spirit*, who also shares the divine nature with Father and Son, but is distinguished from them in some formulations by being neither unbegotten (as is the Father) nor begotten (as is the Son), but by having "proceeded." The distinction of persons is the result of their eternal relations, and, in Augustine's influential conception, the person of the Holy Spirit is regarded as the relation of mutual love that binds together Father and Son. The trinitarian conception is, therefore, a way of characterizing God as a dynamic, living, and personal being whose identity is constituted by a loving relationality in which differences are nonadversarial, indeed mutually life-enhancing. The triune deity is said to have created the cosmos through the *logos* and human beings according to its image (where "image" refers to the Son or *logos*, who is the *image of God* the Father). Human beings are therefore said to "bear the image of God," and their final consummation entails the full recovery or expression of that image (see also divinization under Consummation). Human beings are also said to possess human *spirits*, which in some theological formulations mark their point of engagement with God as Holy Spirit, but which in some literary theoretical formulations represent their wholly independent human natures.

Tropes or "turnings" are words and phrases that turn meaning from one direction (often called the "*literal*") to another. Discussion of tropes (or "figures") was prominent in ancient rhetoric and subsequently infiltrated literary studies, especially the study of poetry. Two important tropes are metaphor and metonymy: a *metaphor* regards one thing as another ("my love is a red, red rose," where rose is a trope for my love); a *metonymy* refers to something by means of a closely associated item or idea (for example, referring to the king as "the crown"). Closely associated with metonymy is *synecdoche*, by which one uses part of a thing to refer to the whole ("here comes a sail," speaking of an approaching ship). An important trope for Bloom is *metalepsis* or *transumption*, a use of language that makes what is actually later in time appear earlier. Trope should not be confused with *topos*, a word meaning "place" and referring originally in rhetoric to a "commonplace," a standard topic of discourse (all funeral orations would, for example, include the *topos* or topic of praise of the deceased's lineage). Bloom uses *topos* to indicate the *stance* or orientation of a poet (*ephebe*, or young man) in a conflict of will (*agon*, or struggle) with his poetic predecessor.

Troping means to read a text in such a way as to turn it into a trope. Troping is therefore a means of *revision* (reseeing): one "tropes" or "tropes upon" a text in order to turn it in a direction different from the one it assumes on its own—in order to see it again in a different light. The Christian figural or *typological* reading of Hebrew Scripture is a kind of troping, which can, for example, turn a text about a historical flight of Israelites from Egypt into an allegory about the spiritual exodus of the soul from sin (see also Conversion). Bloom's *misprision* or *misreading* is a troping by later poets on the texts of their poetic precursors. For de Man, troping can be a means by which readers engage in *recuperation*—that is, create for an inherently meaningless text a simulacrum of meaning (see symbol under Deconstruction). Such recuperative troping does for literary studies what *foundationalism* does for philosophy: it holds out the promise of discovering a bedrock of meaning or truth beneath the shifting sands of language's unstable surface. But according to de Man, both recuperative troping in literature and foundationalism in philosophy fail to recognize language's inescapable *disfiguration*—its violent, "perverse turning" away from any meaning or truth, and back upon itself in an arbitrary act of power.

Index

Abraham (patriarch), 48, 50
Abstraction, Bakhtin on, 111, 112, 113, 114, 115, 122–23. *See also* Theoreticism
Adam, 13, 103, 104
Aesthetics, 14, 54, 56, 72, 75, 79, 85, 87, 91, 98–99, 100–101, 107, 108, 113–17, 118, 122, 137
Aesthetization, 98, 108, 137. *See also* Consummation
Agon, 8, 12, 29, 49, 76-77, 80-81, 100, 144
Allegory, 21, 58, 60, 61–62, 69, 74, 76, 123, 138, 144
Allusions, poetic, in Bloom's theory, 9, 41
Anti-Semitism, 10, 49, 50, 84
The Anxiety of Influence (Bloom), 9, 40, 42
Aphasia, 24–25
Apologetics, 4, 16
Apostles' Creed, 15
Aporia, 12, 34, 37, 38, 42–43, 68, 78–79, 138. *See also* Oscillation; Rhetoricity; Textuality
Aquinas, Thomas, 93, 94, 95
Aristotle, 80
Athanasius, 15, 138
Augustine, 15, 22, 23, 24, 28, 34–39, 45–46, 105–6, 111, 129, 140, 142, 143

"Author and Hero in Aesthetic Activity" (Bakhtin), 11, 87, 89

Bakhtin, Mikhail
  account of his theory, 2, 4–5, 11, 120–24
  compared to Bloom and de Man, 13–14, 86, 88–110
  and incarnation, 5, 123
  and rejection of theoreticism, 119
  his theory as a theology, 118
Baptism, 25, 27, 29, 35, 60. *See also* Sacrament
Barth, Karl, 16–17
Beatific vision, 89, 138
"Before Moses Was, I Am" (Bloom), 48, 52
Benjamin, Walter, 56, 62–69, 107, 123
Bercovitch, Sacvan, 48
Bible, 8, 29, 37, 105, 106, 138. *See also* Hebrew Scripture; New Testament; Old Testament
Blake, William, 45
Bloom, Harold
  account of his theory, 4, 8–9, 10–11, 39–54, 118, 119
  and Bakhtin, 86, 99–110, 121–22

and Christian revisionary reading, 23, 32, 45–54, 69
and de Man, 23, 39–40, 76–77
on the ephebe, 8–9, 12, 13, 41, 44, 45, 48–49, 81, 100, 122
and gnosticism, 133–34 n.81
his relation to Judaism, 23, 46, 48, 49, 51–52
and incarnation, 5, 12, 119
and Martin Luther, 53–54
on relation between Judaism and Christianity, 29, 131 n.68
and Romanticism, 101
and tradition, 101
Body, 5–6, 6–8, 8–14, 44, 45, 57–69, 71, 108
Bultmann, Rudolf, 7
Burke, Kenneth, 3

Camus, Albert, 121
Canon, canonization, 118
Carnivalization, 11, 87
Chalcedonian Creed. *See* Creed of Chalcedon
Chance, and de Man, 13
Christ
  advents of, according to Luther, 25–26
  body of, in Eucharist, 57–69

146